1950

D1393556

# The
# Spanish
# Property
# Guide

All You Need To Know About Property In Spain

**By David Searl**

SANTANA BOOKS

## ACKNOWLEDGEMENTS

We would like to express our deepest gratitude to those people who took time from their busy workdays in government offices, private practice of professsions, and on through a long list, to answer our questions.

Special thanks go to:

Lawyer Manuel Ubeda Castañeda of Ubeda-Retana y Asociados legal services in Fuengirola for the answers to many, many questions, and the questions that arose from the questions.

Lawyer and Tax Consultant Jorge Retana, also of Ubeda-Retana, for a thorough knowledge of Spanish tax legislation affecting foreigners.

Tax Consultant Sergio Llull, also of Ubeda-Retana, for special expertise in dealing with Spain's Tax Agency.

Gestor Ricardo Bocanegra of Marbella for sharing his long experience working with foreigners.

**THE SPANISH PROPERTY GUIDE**  is published by:

Ediciones Santana S.L.,

Apartado 422,  29640 Fuengirola (Málaga), Spain.

Tel 952 485 838. Fax 952 485 367.

E-mail santana@net.es

First Santana edition published in October 1998.
Second edition, March 2000.

Design and typesetting by Jon Harper.

Imprime Gráficas San Pancracio S.L.,

Poligono Industrial San Luis,

Calle Orotava 17, Málaga, Spain.

Deposito Legal : MA-227/2000      ISBN  84–89954–05–4

# The
# Spanish Property Guide

## Contents

# INTRODUCTION

If you want to buy property in Spain, you will be in good company. Estimates are that more than one million foreigners already own their primary residence or a second home in the Spanish sun.

These sunshine properties line the Mediterranean coasts from Barcelona to Algeciras, and continue around the Atlantic corner at Gibraltar to Cadiz province.

The Balearic Islands, especially Mallorca, are dotted with British and German holiday homes, as well as the villas of retirees.

The Canary Islands offer their own particular charm, with full time residents not quite catching up to timeshare owners but gradually gaining ground.

In spite of Europe's unemployment problems, there is a climate of prosperity in the air, and sales of Spanish property are setting records in all areas, with the British and Germans leading the way.

On the Costa del Sol alone, it is estimated that as many as 200,000 homes are already owned by foreigners, and the rate of foreign investment in real estate has steadily risen for the last several years. In 1999 it was more than 90,000 million pesetas — almost 500 million pounds — and the rate was rising towards the records of the 1989 property boom. On the Costa Blanca sales totalled more than 60,000 million pesetas.

Furthermore, prices have begun to rise, with Málaga province showing an increase of about 10 per cent in general, while hot areas like Marbella jumped sharply, about 20 per cent for 1999. Part of this increase has to do with rising standards of construction. Today's buyers of Spanish homes are looking for truly European quality, and the builders are now offering it.

Today's buyers are also looking for homes in the sun to enjoy for themselves and their families. They are not the speculators looking for quick profits who created the boom of the late1980s.

The vast bulk of the unfinished properties that littered the landscape on the Costa Blanca and Costa del Sol have now been sold off, many of them at bargain prices, during the lean years, and new construction is well underway.

In the more prestigious areas such as Marbella and parts of the Balearic Islands, the problem in fact is concern about overbuilding.

The Marbella Town Plan, which has drawn sharp criticism and which still awaits final approval from the Andalusian planning board, foresees that the municipality will more than triple its population by the year 2005, meaning that about 8,000 homes must be built every year. The vast majority of these will be holiday homes in urbanizations.

Many of the new buyers have been attracted by the improvement in public services, including rubbish, sewage, police protection, cleaner beaches, more and better roads, but concerned residents fear that another population boom will set off what they call the "Torremolinos" syndrome, meaning that every green space will be covered with concrete and even the new services will not be able to keep up.

In the Balearics, authorities are discussing the possibility of limiting further tourist development, in order to maintain the character of the islands, and similar situations apply all over the Spanish costas.

Nevertheless, most homeowners and holidaymakers would rather deal with the problems of growth and prosperity than the problems of poverty and neglect, and those prospective buyers who are really looking for a country retreat in the sunshine will find that enormous inland areas behind the Mediterranean beaches are now opening up, with farms and country properties readily available near the still-unspoilt white villages of the interior.

Prosperity and growth also mean that your holiday home is likely to increase in value over the years. Experts predict that prices will continue to rise, even if not as sharply as in 1999.

Regardless of the type of Spanish property you choose, or the area you prefer for your holidays or retirement, you will face an unfamiliar set of rules and regulations, in a language which you probably don't know. Spanish property laws and taxes are not the same as British or German laws.

Even though the free-swinging days of the property boom have ended, when buyers were throwing money at sellers who often did not have clear titles, we still see situations where unscrupulous dealers will write unfavourable terms into contracts and take advantage of the ignorant foreigner.

A little preparation in advance can save you time, trouble and money in the future.

This book sets out the basic rules, laws and practices of Spanish property transactions for buying, selling, renting, letting and the leasing of commercial premises as well. We will see that practice sometimes differs from the law as it is written. We will also see that old-timers and insiders will try to tell you that some practices are accepted which are not and which will cause you, the buyer, serious problems later.

Did you know that, because of recent changes in tax regulations, every non-resident who buys a property today will be liable for Spanish capital gains tax of 35 per cent on his profit when he later sells? The old exemption from tax after 10 years of ownership has disappeared.

Did you know that the former Spanish practice of under-declaring the amount of a sale in order to minimise transfer taxes is no longer workable?

Did you know that Spain's finance ministry will set its own valuation on a property transfer and you, the buyer, will not find out until six months later? By that time, the seller may be long gone and you will be liable for additional taxes on the sale.

Did you know that, unless you are very careful in letting your property, you can be stuck with a "short-term" tenant for five years, with only limited rental increases each year?

These and many other useful tips will be found in this book. Nevertheless, the book cannot be a substitute for individual professional advice. Do not attempt to be your own lawyer. And if your seller offers to handle all the legal details for you, politely decline his offer. You cannot expect the other party to look after your interests as well as his own, can you?

Use a Spanish lawyer or other property professional when you buy property in Spain. If you already own property and you intend to sell it, use a lawyer or a tax consultant.

Figure about one per cent of the value of the transaction for a lawyer's fee, as an example. Some charge more, few charge less.

A little money spent now can save you unpleasant surprises later.

# CONTENTS

# Buying Property

You're right. You should have bought a holiday home or a retirement residence in Spain two years ago. Depending on the area, you would have seen an average 30 per cent rise in the value of your property, perhaps more.

Do not despair. Experts predict that prices of Spanish property will continue to rise for the immediate future, and that they certainly will not drop. This means that you are still in time to make a sensible purchase that will bring you pleasure and keep your investment safe.

Furthermore, you have a wide choice available to you now, on all the Spanish coasts. New construction of high quality is booming all over Spain and particularly in the Mediterranean areas. Spanish property sellers are also giving prospective purchasers good terms and more professional service.

Property experts all agree that the introduction of the Euro will benefit the purchase of holiday homes and the unsettled stock market will make real estate look like a better investment than before, so your Spanish property will almost certainly increase in value over the years.

Finally, mortgage rates, at around 6 per cent, are at record lows although they are expected to rise soon.

But the foreign buyer needs to take care. Too many purchasers seem to leave their brains at the airport when they enter Spain.

You need sound legal advice from a Spanish professional who may be a lawyer, a registered estate agent, a specialized *gestor,* or an *administrador de fincas,* any of whom is qualified to act in your interests and make sure you are protected and well-advised in the transaction. It's foolish to depend entirely on the seller of the property to make sure you are treated fairly.

Let's give the basic "Buyer Beware" warning first. It goes like this: Believe Nothing. Check Everything.

When they say there is no outstanding mortgage, check the Property Registry. When they say it measures 145 square metres, measure it. When they say the terrace is included, check the plans.

Any reputable seller will be perfectly happy to have his offers checked.

This section will advise buyers on how to make legal checks of many points in their purchase.

Both the European Union and the Spanish government have investigated fraud reports in holiday property, revealing the presence of illegal urbanisations where unwary buyers end up having problems of unpaid taxes, unregistered title deeds, and difficulty in obtaining municipal services or building permission. Spaniards themselves have been defrauded as well, and problems with house purchase make up a principal area of complaint for the Spanish consumers associations.

A few of these illegal and unregistered urbanizations, especially in Alicante province, were started on beach land with no planning permission or building permits. When authorities moved to crack down on illegal building, threatening expropriation and demolition after a 30-year grace period, sensation-seeking British newspapers claimed that all holiday properties were menaced by strict new laws for coastal protection. Not so. In fact, the estates and buildings in question had been in violation of several laws for many years, and the authorities had finally caught up with them.

### *Ley de Costas:*

Spain's 1988 *Ley de Costas,* or Law of Coasts, does in fact empower the authorities to restrict building and to control height and density within 100 metres of the high-water mark, and it establishes a "zone of influence" as far inland as one kilometre. A small number of illegally-built villas, apartments and beach bars were in fact ordered to be torn down, but these violated even the provisions of earlier laws, as well as town planning regulations.

Other properties continue to be built near the beach, as they are approved under the terms of the new law, which does not end beachfront building.

### *Plan Parcial:*

To make sure your urbanization is legal and registered, ask to see the *plan parcial* approved by the *urbanismo* department of your *Ayuntamiento,* or town hall. The *urbanismo* office is the department of town planning. The *plan parcial* is not a partial plan, as it sounds, but the plan of *parcelas,* or building plots, which must be approved. This assures you that your urbanization is legal. If the developer cannot show you the approved *plan parcial,* you may have a problem. If it is on the beach, make sure that the development is approved by the *Jefatura de Costas* as well as the Town Hall. Do not buy near the beach without seeing the authorization from the Coast department.

Even then, other problems can arise. Are you *sure* the company which has just sold you a half-finished apartment is solvent enough to complete the promised building? Do you *really* know what back taxes may be due on the lovely villa you have just signed for?

There are steps you can take to check these points and we shall discuss them below.

### Real Estate Agent

But let's start at the beginning. Your first contact when you decide to buy property in Spain will almost certainly be the estate agent, or many estate agents.

In many countries, an estate agent is a registered professional who can be held financially responsible if he intermediates in a sale and the terms later turn out to be falsely based.

In Spain this is also true on paper, but in practice, it much more difficult to hold an estate agent, even a registered one, responsible when a purchase goes wrong. Citizens of Scandinavian countries, or the UK, for example, where consumers are most carefully protected, even from their own mistakes, should be a little more wary in Spain.

If your Spanish estate agent causes you to suffer loss, either through negligence or honest error, you will have a hard time obtaining any recompense. Ask your agent if he carries Professional Indemnity Insurance, and, if so, how much. You may again be surprised to find that most estate agents have either no insurance at all or a minimum amount required by the official Spanish agent's association. Ask your agent if he operates a Bonded Client's Account, into which any deposits you make will be placed, and which is untouchable except for the stated purpose of the deposit. If you suffer any loss, you will be reimbursed.

## Take Care with Deposit

Here is what can happen if you pay your deposit directly to the seller.

In December of 1997 a British couple found a villa they liked on the Costa del Sol. They agreed a price of 30 million pesetas, and in January of 1998 they transferred a deposit of three million pesetas, 10 per cent, to reserve the villa from its German owners.

The British couple used a Spanish lawyer plus the advice of a British property agent working in Spain and they felt all was well. The couple sold their home in the UK, shipped their furniture to Spain, wound up their business, and came to Spain for the April closing of the sale, when they would pay the rest of the price and sign the deed.

Just before the date with the Notary, their lawyer received a message from the German sellers, saying they could not make it that day and that they would be in touch later. This set off alarm bells with everybody involved. It turned out that the owners had in fact sold the property a month earlier for 35 million pesetas to another buyer, had kept the three million pesetas deposited with them, and had left Spain for parts unknown.

Of course our unfortunate British buyers have a clear case against the German sellers for breach of contract, with the right to recover their deposit, plus damages and loss, but how are they going to find them? In fact they have the right to a sum twice the amount of the deposit if their agreement is correctly worded and the seller backs out of the deal.

In many European countries, the buyers would also have a case against the estate agent and perhaps the lawyer as well for negligence in performing their services. In Spain they also have a case but where standards are less strict and where the lawyer and estate agent declare that they simply followed accepted practice and were just as dismayed as their clients, a Spanish court might well accept their arguments.

So, be sure to take care that any deposit you make goes into that escrow account, a blocked account, where neither party can get at it until the sale is closed.

Even though the results were not good in this instance, this case and others like it make a powerful argument for using a Spanish lawyer when you buy property. I will say it again and again. You should use a Spanish lawyer when you buy property in Spain. You should use a lawyer in your own country when you buy property. Why should it be different in Spain?

One reason for this is because you yourself do not know your way around in Spain. Innocent foreigners have fallen victim to cowboy property sellers simply because they speak the victim's own language. That is, Germans tend to be tricked by fellow-Germans and Brits tend to fall prey to other Britons, who win their confidence and say that in Spain everything is different, but don't worry, he, the cowboy, will handle everything. This can lead to the simplest and most devastating type of fraud, where the "agent" himself gives the buyer a contract only in English, takes the money himself, and disappears, leaving the poor buyer with neither money nor property, because, although the "agent" had the key, he was never authorised to sell the property. The English contract he gave the buyer is worth nothing anyway, because the real owner never signed it. So, use a Spanish lawyer and be safer, if not totally safe.

Having stated this warning, we find that most Spanish estate agents, or foreigners selling property in Spain, are both registered and honest. They only want to make a fair commission by selling good properties which will make their buyers and sellers both happy. Be careful anyway.

A Spanish estate agent can be registered in two ways, either as an API or a GIPE.

The traditional estate agent is licensed as an *Agente de la Propiedad Inmobiliaria,* an API. This for many years was the only official and legally authorised body, and an agent had to belong to the College of Agents in order to qualify.

Newcomers to the property market, who were irritated by the closed-shop attitude of the API, came up with the legal figure of GIPE, which began as a licenced maintenance and sales person in property administration, but expanded itself into sales.

After long legal battles, the GIPE is also accepted as a real estate agent today.

During these same legal battles, the monopoly of the College of API was severely weakened, and now it is not a legal requirement that a person selling property be a member of either institute.

However, you, the buyer, will have a lot more protection if you deal with an API or a GIPE. Ask your estate agent if they are members. These bodies at least maintain some standards for their member agents, and you can complain to them if you have not been fairly treated.

Spain has all sorts of estate agents, ranging from the small office in the High Street, who has been in the town for many years and knows everybody personally, to the most modern international real estate offices, filled with computers, who can contact their office in Frankfurt or London by Internet, and screen you five views of their offerings right there on the computer. In addition, there are many "Euro agents" of all nationalities who quite legally operate in Spain, although their credentials may not be as well-established.

Most Europeans will be surprised to find that estate agents dealing with Spanish holiday property take commissions starting at five per cent and going up to 10 per cent. These high commissions, say the agents, are justified because they have to deal with many unusual factors in a market where people are of different nationalities and where Spanish regulations make all transactions more complicated than necessary. Let's just say that, when you are in the final stages of negotiating your purchase price, even the amount of the estate agent's commission might come on the table for a little reduction.

One of these agents should be able to find the property you are looking for. Very few agents in Spain are exclusive, so you might find two agents showing you the same property.

Keep in mind that the estate agent is working for the seller, so his presentation of the property will be the most favourable one, and you should check the facts carefully through your own representative. A reputable estate agent will be very happy to have you verify any of his information through your own lawyer, for example.

How to find a good Spanish lawyer? Good question. Here is perhaps the only area in which you can ask advice from people you know. Ask around until you find some satisfied clients.

This is perhaps the only situation in which you can get the right advice by walking into a bar and asking the people if anyone knows a good lawyer. Everybody in the place will have a story about either a good lawyer or a bad one.

Consulates also maintain lists of lawyers who speak the language of their nationality, English, German, and so on. These lists do not mean that the lawyers are the most highly regarded.

How much will it cost? Figure the lawyer to charge you around one per cent of the value of the transaction, unless there are some unusual complications. Settle this with him before you start.

## Before You Sign Anything

Before you sign anything in Spain, even a small reservation deposit agreement, there are some pieces of paper you should see. These include:

1.  The seller's own title, known as the *Escritura Publica*
2.  The paid-up receipt for his annual property tax, the IBI.
3.  The Catastral Certificate giving the boundaries and square metres of area.
4.  Paid-up receipts for Community of Property Owners fees, the Statutes of the Community, and the minutes of the last AGM.

Other documents are important as well and we shall list them.

### *1. Escritura Publica*

The *Escritura Publica* is the registered title deed of the property. It is inscribed in the *Registro de la Propiedad,* the Property Registry, and it is the only ironclad guarantee of title in Spain. If your seller cannot produce an *escritura publica*, something is wrong. In this title deed you will find a description of the property, the details of the owner, and, if any mortgages or court embargoes exist against the property, they will be registered here as marginal notes. You want to see the seller's title deed, if only to make sure that he really is the owner of the property being sold to you. Your lawyer can obtain a *nota simple* from the Registry, containing the pertinent details and notes of any mortgages. However, it would be best if you could see a copy of the complete deed.

Strange things can happen with deeds. In one recent case, a widow was selling her property in Spain. However, living in another country, it had never occurred to her to declare the death of her husband in Spain, and his name was still entered on the title deed as half owner of the property. This had been done in perfect innocence, because she simply considered herself the full owner of the property when her husband died.

By Spanish law a property held jointly in two names cannot be sold without the signatures of both parties. Because no one had seen the full *escritura* before the scheduled closing and final payment, the fact did not come to light until both parties were ready to sign at the Spanish Notary. The signing had to be postponed for months until the widow could declare her husband's death, which had happened 10 years before, prove that she was the heir, formally accept the inheritance, re-register the property in her own name, and finally sign to sell it. One fortunate consequence of her error was that she did not have to pay any Spanish inheritance tax, because the demand for the tax lapses after five years. Some people do this deliberately, but her lack of action was inadvertent.

All this inheritance settlement could have taken place early in the negotiations if the title deed had been available for examination. You will do well to insist on seeing the complete *escritura*. It's a good idea to know that the seller is really the owner of the property, after all.

## 2. Check IBI Receipt

One very important paper you must see before purchasing any Spanish property is the *Impuesto sobre Bienes Inmuebles* (IBI), the municipal real estate tax. When purchasing a new flat or house, it is your responsibility to make sure that the house is registered for this tax, and when purchasing from the second or third owner, you must always ask to see the latest paid-up receipt for the IBI before you sign any contract with the seller. If he doesn't have it, you may find yourself liable for back taxes and penalties. Here again your lawyer or property consultant will have valuable advice.

The IBI receipt will show the property's catastral reference number and also your *valor catastral,* the official assessed value of the property. This is a very important figure because various taxes are based on it. (See section on You and Your Taxes). The assessed value is almost always considerably less than the real market value, but has been steadily raised over the last few years.

THE SPANISH PROPERTY GUIDE

Your annual real estate tax is charged by the municipality, and it can be as low as 20,000 pesetas if you own a small cottage in one of the typical villages, or as much as 300,000 pesetas a year if you own a new luxury villa on acres of land near Marbella.

A surcharge of 20 per cent will be placed on the bill if it is not paid on time. Often, you can arrange to have this bill paid directly through your bank, in order to avoid forgetting it. You fill out the forms authorizing the bank to pay it, and the tax people will send the bill directly to the bank. In many municipalities those who pay their IBI tax early get discounts of 10 per cent, and a standing order at the bank will ensure that this is done.

So when buying an older property, whether apartment or villa, you want to see the last IBI receipt. If not available, something is amiss. Really, you want to see the IBI receipts for the last five years, not just the current one, because you can be liable for five years of back tax.

The current IBI receipt must be presented to the Notary at the signing of the contract, because it contains the catastral reference number, but you as the buyer want to see it well before that.

### 3. Referencia Catastral

As of 1997, every property sale must include a mention of the *Referencia Catastral*. As noted above, this reference number appears on your IBI receipt.

The Catastro is a second system of property registration, concentrating on the exact location, physical description and boundaries of property, unlike the Property Registry, which focuses on ownership and title. The Catastro is also concerned with the valuation of property and is the source of the famous *valor catastral*, the assessed value of property for tax purposes. (See IBI section for more details).

These two systems, strangely enough, have never even communicated with each other, and we find that the catastral description of a property sometimes differs greatly from the one in the Property Registry, which makes no sense.

As a first step in trying to bring the physical reality into line with statements people sometimes make in contracts, the Spanish authorities have begun to require that all property transactions now include at least a mention of the Catastro reference number in addition to the *escritura*.

It is a very good idea for the buyer to request the actual certification from the Catastro with a full description of the property. If it matches the data given in your contract, you are all right. If there are large differences, perhaps something is wrong.

The certification itself comes in two parts, one being a description in words of the property and the other being a graphic representation, either a plan or an aerial photo. Get both of them. It costs only a few pounds, although it can take up to two months for the Catastro to deliver the certificates, so you had better start early.

It is astonishing how often the boundaries and square metres of a property can differ so much. This is because people simply accept the statements made in the title deed, and do not check any further. Be warned that, when you ask the seller or the estate agent for this catastral certificate, they will pooh-pooh the idea, saying it is not legally necessary yet, although it will be in the future. Do not pay much attention to them. Insist on getting it, so you can be sure of your real boundaries and the real size of the property.

The Notary is also empowered to call attention to the fact that discrepancies exist between the Catastro and Property Registry descriptions.

The buyer and seller can go ahead with their transaction, but they have been advised of the discrepancy.

## 4. Community Fees, Statutes and Minutes of AGM

If you are buying a flat, a townhouse, or a villa on an urbanization, ask also to see the latest paid-up receipt for community fees. These are the fees charged by your *Comunidad de Propietarios,* the Community of Property Owners, which is the Spanish term for "condominium", meaning the legal body that controls all the elements held in common. In a building this would be the lift, gardens and pool for example. In an urbanization, the Community as a whole jointly owns the roads, gardens, pool, lighting system and other elements as well. Each owner is assigned a quota, or percentage of the expenses, which he must pay, by law. See the section on Communities for full details. Just remember that you become a member of the Community, with legal rights and obligations, just by purchasing your property. Only those who buy a country property or a house on a normal street in a town will not have to deal with Community problems.

The receipt for Community fees assures you that the fees are paid and gives you a good idea of your monthly charges in the future.

Read the Statutes of the community, too, as they will be binding on you once you have signed the purchase contract. If the basic Statutes that rule the Community prohibit the keeping of pets in the building or on the estate, you will have real problems if you want to keep your dogs, for example. Get a copy of these Statutes in a language you can read, even if the Spanish regulations are the only valid ones.

Then you want to see the Minutes Book, the official record, of the last Annual General Meeting of the Community. Decisions are taken by majority vote of the owners at each year's AGM, and these actions are recorded in the Minutes Book, which is an official document. If you find that the principal point at last year's meeting was how to solve the Community's chronic water shortage, then you will know you are going to have problems in your new house. Talk to the President of the Community if this is possible. A well-run Community can add millions of pesetas to a property's value, and a Community with problems is a source of endless aggravation.

### *Declaración de Obra Nueva*

In the case of a new property, you want to make sure that the property has been declared to Hacienda for IBI, as you can incur more fines for not registering it. Make sure that your developer has made a *declaración de obra nueva,* a declaration of new building, and has paid the small tax associated with this, as well. Make sure that your *escritura* mentions the house you have purchased as well as the plot of land on which it stands. Sometimes the deed only refers to the land. This makes you the owner of anything standing on the land, of course, but you may find yourself subject to taxes and fines relating to an undeclared building.

Sometimes, the purchase of an undeclared building can even work in your favour, but you will need expert advice to make sure you stay within the law.

Remember that the seller decided not to register his house in order to avoid paying the taxes due on this declaration of new construction.

Some buyers, faced with this circumstance, make a contract to purchase only the land from the seller. That's all he has title to, anyway. The price for the land alone is much lower than the price for the land and house together, for a considerable saving on the property transfer tax of 6 per cent. You purchase the house separately by a private contract. Then the new buyer makes the *declaración de obra nueva,* just as if he himself has built the house. Building permits and other papers are necessary for this, but it can all be arranged, and the buyer will pay only one half of one per cent, compared to the transfer tax of 6 per cent. It has been done but sound legal advice should be taken because the plan will not work in all areas and situations.

### *Plan Parcial*

If you are buying on an urbanization, you want to have a look at that *plan parcial,* the plan of parcels or plots of land, registered with the *Urbanismo,* or town planning department of your Town Hall. This assures you that the urbanization itself is registered and legal. If it isn't, you may have problems later with your Community, with municipal services such as light and water, and obtaining from the contractor all the elements promised in your sale. It is also important to have a look at the Town Planning maps of the area around you. A newly prosperous Spain is improving the road system all around the country. What if one of those highways is planned for the bottom of your garden? You can find out from the town's urban plan. If you yourself cannot read plans, and few of us can, have your lawyer do it.

## Utilities Receipts

And, of course, you want to see paid-up receipts for the owner's electricity, water, rubbish collection, and even telephone. This assures you that the bills are paid and also gives you an idea of what it will cost to run the place.

One small note on electric or light bills: If you wind up stuck with unpaid bills by the previous owner, be aware that these are personal bills from private companies. They do not attach to the property, only to the person who signed the electric or water company contract. The company will insist that they will cut off the service if the bills are not paid. Let them cut it off. For a reasonable fee, you simply go into the company office and sign a new contract, starting fresh without the previous owner's bills.

Once you and your lawyer or adviser are satisfied with these checks, you and the seller can begin thinking about the terms of the contract. Keep in mind that you must factor into your calculations the amount of taxes and fees that will be paid on the transaction.

## Transfer Taxes and Fees: 10%

What are the taxes and fees going to cost you? They will probably be less than 10 per cent of the purchase price if the breaks are with you, but can go as high as 15 per cent if certain taxes turn out to be higher than usual in your individual case.

You have two taxes and two fees to pay on the transfer of property. The two fees are for the notarization of the deed and for its registry in the property registry. The two taxes are the transfer tax and a sort of capital gains tax on the increase in value of the land, usually called the *plus valía* tax.

## Notary

You pay the *notario* a fee fixed by an official scale. The fee varies according to the amount of land, the size of the dwelling and its price, but let's say between 50,000 and 70,000 pesetas.

## Property Registry

Then there is a fee for the registry of the property in the official *Registro de la Propiedad*. This will be a similar amount. Your lawyer or property consultant can tell you exactly how much these fees will be before you buy.

## Transfer Tax

The transfer tax, called *Impuesto de Transmisiones Patrimoniales* in Spanish, is 6 per cent of the value declared in the contract. This ITP is charged on private sales. If you purchase from a property company, this tax will be IVA (value added tax), at 7 per cent because the sale is a business operation, not a private deal between two individuals. In addition to this, you pay a documents fee, or stamp duty, of one half of one per cent, so buying a new property will draw tax of 7.5 per cent.

There is one more tax to which you should be alerted. This is the *plus valía* tax, a municipal charge, which the seller is supposed to pay. If he does not, however, it can be charged against the property itself, meaning that you as the new owner will have to pay it. We discuss this in detail below.

## How Much to Declare?

Formerly it was the practice to declare a ridiculously low amount for the value of the house, in order to minimize this tax, but now Spanish lawyers advise sellers and buyers to declare the approximate market value, normally the real value of the sale. Spanish tax inspectors will come around and make their own assessment if they feel the declaration is too low. Spain's Tax Agency maintains its own tables of values on property, and they are empowered to set a higher value on a sale if they judge the declaration to be under market value. More than one property purchaser has been disconcerted to discover that he has to pay some extra taxes when he gets their bill six months after the sale.

If they discover that the transfer has been under-declared by more than two million pesetas and 20 per cent, they can apply heavy penalties to both the buyer and seller under the terms of Spain's 1989 *Ley de Tasas* — the law of public fees — which was enacted to prevent precisely this dodge.

Another point to keep in mind is that, when you go to resell your property, you will be charged Spanish capital gains tax on any profit you make. You will pay as part of your income tax (as a resident) with a maximum of 20 per cent, or the 35 per cent capital gains tax (as a non-resident) on the profits you have made, so if you declare a low value now, you will be liable for tax on a much bigger profit when you sell later. (See section on "You and Your Taxes" for more details.)

As a final note, you can ask the tax office what value they will accept on any particular property. Inquire at the *oficina liquidadora,* the payment office, at your nearest Hacienda office, and they will tell you exactly what value they assign to your purchase. They base their valuation on a careful study of various factors, such as location, size, quality, age, and others. Or just do as most people are doing today, and declare the actual amount of the sale.

### *Plus Valía*

The other tax on property sales is the *arbitrio sobre el incremento del valor de los terrenos,* the tax on the increase in the value of the land since its last sale. This is usually called the *plus valía* for short, and it can vary widely. In the case of an apartment or a townhouse in a new urbanization, where little land is involved and where there has been no real increase in value because such a short time has passed since it was developed, the tax can be very low. It will be much higher if you buy a house with several thousand square metres of land, which has not changed hands for 20 years and which has been recently re-zoned from rural to urban land, thus jumping greatly in value.

This tax is based on the official value of the land, which is always lower than the market value, and it varies from 10 per cent up to 40 per cent of the annual increase, depending on the length of time between sales and the town where it is located. The land is officially revalued periodically for this purpose.

Do not confuse this *plus valía* tax with the non-resident's 35 per cent capital gains tax on profits from the sale.

You can find out exactly how much your *plus valía* will be simply by going into the municipal tax office in your town and asking. They keep the records there for each property and will be glad to tell you the assessed value, so you can find out in advance. Or have your lawyer or property consultant do it.

These are the two taxes and two fees you will have to pay.

**Who Pays What?**

The first and most important point to make here is that the buyer and seller are free to contract whatever terms they choose. There is no Spanish law which requires that one of the parties must pay any particular tax.

The second important point is that, since January 1, 1999, the *plus valía* tax can be charged directly against the property itself, meaning that an unscrupulous seller might promise to pay it, then "forget" to pay it, leaving the new owner stuck with the tax, or losing his property.

Traditionally, the seller has paid the notary's fees and the *plus valía* tax, as he, after all, is the one making the profit on the increase in the land's value, and for the buyer to pay the *impuesto de transmisiones* and the registry fee, as he is the one who is interested in making sure the property is truly registered to his name.

It has now become a frequent practice, however, for the contract to state that the buyer will pay *todos los gastos,* all the expenses arising. There is nothing illegal about this.

Remember that the two parties are free to make any contract they choose.

This practice, which may seem unfair to the buyer, has come about because tax bills, especially the *plus valía,* have often gone unpaid, especially by non-resident sellers. By the time the new purchaser realized this, the seller was gone and the buyer stuck with the taxes anyway, as they were billed to the owner of the property if the seller did not pay. Charging the new owner with all the taxes is at least straightforward and avoids complications.

Nevertheless, you can use this point in negotiating your final price. If the contract you are offered states that you as the purchaser must pay all taxes and fees, you could suggest that the seller take something off the price.

Finally, you have your lawyer's fee, or the fee to the *administrador de fincas* or *gestor* who has advised you. A lawyer's fee may be as little as 50,000 pesetas if he has merely vetted your contract, found it good, handled the basic paperwork and encountered no complications. It can be much higher if the *abogado* discovers that your seller has no *escritura* of his own, which often happens on the Spanish coast because property is so rapidly transferred from hand to hand, or if he has to sort out other complications, such as taxes that haven't been paid.

As a rough guide, figure one per cent of the price as a standard lawyer's fee

## The Contract

Let's suppose that you have found a property that suits you, that all of the pre-purchase checks have satisfied you, and you have negotiated the price down to what you can pay. Keep in mind that very few sellers will not come down on the price. Make an offer and see what happens.

Once you have decided that you can pay for it, your next concern is the sales contract.

Because most buyers take some time to assemble the cash needed for the purchase, it is usual for the buyer and seller to make a "private contract" first, with the buyer putting down a non-returnable deposit of, say 10 per cent. This reserves the property while the buyer brings his money into Spain or perhaps obtains a Spanish mortgage. If the buyer fails to complete the sale, he loses the amount of his deposit.

If the seller finds another buyer in the meantime, willing to pay more, and sells the property, the first offerer can claim twice the amount of the deposit back.

Remember never to pay the deposit directly to the seller. Make sure that it goes into an escrow account, a blocked account, called a Bonded Client Account, from which it will not be released until the sale is final. Insist on this.

The seller, through the estate agent, will certainly have a draft private contract all ready for you to sign. The contract they offer may suit you perfectly, but it is quite likely that it will contain some clauses more favourable to the seller than to you, the buyer. This is when you want your lawyer to read the contract and make suggestions.

It is a very good idea to have the contract made in Spanish, with a translation into English or German or your native language, so you can be absolutely sure about what you are signing.

This private contract, although it sets out all the details of the agreement, such as payment terms and who pays what share of the taxes, is not the final document for the sale.

This final document is the *escritura de compraventa* and it must be signed by you and the seller in the presence of a Spanish *notario* in order to make it legally binding. You can make a *poder* — a power of attorney — allowing another person to sign for you if you cannot be present. The *notario,* or notary, is an official of the State who makes sure that contracts are legal. He keeps the original document in his files in case any question arises later. The *notario* is a public official, not a private lawyer. His duty is to certify that the contract has been signed, the money paid, and that the purchaser and seller have been advised of their tax obligations. He does not verify or guarantee the accuracy of the statements made in the contract. He only certifies that the parties have signed it properly. Too many people think that the *notario* assures them that all statements made in the contract are true. This is not so. The Notary can, however, give useful advice to both parties.

Let's take these points one by one. First, the contract.

If you cannot read the Spanish contract — the only valid one — you ought to get a copy in English or in a language you can understand. The foreign private contract you sign with an English company promoting property sales is perfectly valid in its country of origin, but it does not make you the absolute owner of any property in Spain, regardless of what the salesman tells you. Only the *compraventa*, in Spanish, signed before a Spanish notary, will do that.

## Title and Registration

In fact, even the *escritura de compraventa* contract does not fully assure your title until it is registered with the Spanish Property Registry, thus making it an *escritura publica,* a public document. It is, in fact, the same document, now registered and with the stamps of the *Registro de la Propiedad* on it.

As of 1997, a notice of the contract signed can be sent by fax directly from the notary's office, at the time of signing, to the *Registro de la Propiedad.* This notification will ensure that no one else can register the property, until the full contract is presented at the Registry.

Or you can have someone deliver the signed contract directly to the Registry. Normally, this will be someone from the notary's office.

This is because, unlike in the UK for example, you yourself will never have the original of your *escritura publica.* The original document is stamped at the Property Registry, which converts it from a sales contract into a public document, the famous *escritura publica,* which is your final and definite title, proof against all comers.

The document is then returned to the Notary, where it is kept safely on file. If you, or any official body, needs a copy of it, you request it from the Notary, who produces an authorised copy. The copy is what you take home.

The reason for haste in delivering the sales contract to the Property Registry is simple. As long as the property continues to be registered in the name of the seller, he can use it to take out a mortgage, for example. The bank checks the Registry, finds the property correctly listed, and grants the seller a mortgage of, say, 20 million pesetas on the villa valued at 30 million pesetas. Our criminally-minded seller has prepared this operation well in advance with the innocent bank, but he does not execute it until after the sale has taken place, in the time interval between signing the *compra-venta* contract and your registration of it as an *escritura publica*.

Otherwise, you see, you would have found the mortgage listed in the Property Registry when you got your *nota simple*. This is also why it is a good idea to get your *nota simple* immediately before you sign the contract.

The seller then disappears to some other country with the 20 million pesetas.

You yourself are perfectly happy with your new property. You are convinced that your pre-purchase checks assured you that the title had no charges against it, which was true at the time.

**Property Sold at Auction**

That is, you are happy for a few years, when you suddenly discover that your property has been sold at auction — *subasta* — without you having been informed, and the police are coming with a court order to put you in the street.

How can this be? The bank which is foreclosing the unpaid mortgage of 20 million pesetas and repossessing the property, will inform only the registered owner, which at the time of making the mortgage was the person who sold it to you. The court has no reason to inform you because you did not exist as far as they are concerned. They are repossessing the house of the person who failed to pay the mortgage. These cases have happened.

Or you might find out about the mortgage because the bank in fact checks at the house and finds you there instead of the mortgage-holder.

You protest that you have nothing to do with this situation, but, legally, you have no case. The bank acted in good faith and their mortgage claim has preference. Your only choice is whether to pay 20 million pesetas more or to abandon the property. You can then, of course, bring suit against the seller to recover your money. If you can find him.

Such cases are rare, but they happen.

Fifty innocent German buyers of apartments near Málaga stand to lose their flats, which they bought in good faith, unless they pay the mortgages outstanding on them.

The Spanish seller, acting through a German agent, who is not implicated, sold the 50 flats in 1990 at good prices in the real estate slump. The German buyers were assured that immediate registration was not necessary. After all, if they did not immediately register their properties with the Property Registry, they did not have to pay the transfer tax.

The seller then took out a mortgage of 70 million pesetas, with the flats as security. Yes, he had already sold them, but the German buyers had failed to obtain the *escritura publica* by registering their flats. This meant that the seller's name still figured on the flats in the Property Registry, so he got his mortgage on them.

He then used the money for other purposes. After some years, the law caught up with the situation, and this seller has been found guilty of fraud. The cheated buyers of course have the right to sue him for the return of their money and any damages they have suffered. However, he has no money to make good the mortgages, so the German buyers will have to pay up or lose their flats to the bank, even though they have the fraudulent seller dead to rights.

This is why it is important to register the deed immediately.

Contracts can be quite simple or very complicated. If you are paying one lump sum and the property is to be delivered at once, there remains only the question of who is to pay the taxes and fees, which are often laid entirely on the purchaser, although this is contrary to Spanish consumer laws and you can negotiate, as we noted above.

If you are paying over a period of time, there will be a number of further provisions in your contract, relating to the timing and amount of the payments.

When paying in stages, the buyer may find that the seller offers him a contract which states that he loses all sums paid out if he fails to keep up the payments, as well as having to vacate the property immediately. In fact, this is always negotiable. If a buyer who cannot keep up the payments will take his case to court, he will find that the court will almost certainly allow him to receive some of his money back in exchange for vacating the property, which he loses.

This will depend on how many payments the buyer has already made, for example. If he has already paid more than half of the full price, the court will not allow the seller to keep it all.

The contract must accurately describe the property being sold. This is one area where the catastral certificate is important. Too many buyers have discovered too late that their boundaries are not what they thought, and the hedgerow at the bottom of their garden, an obvious division, is not the legal line at all, but belongs to their neighbour. This sort of error does not necessarily imply bad faith on the part of the seller. He may have happily accepted the boundaries and square metres set out in his title deed, and never checked them, and thinks he is selling you the bottom part of the garden. Remember that we mentioned the *Registro de la Propiedad* is concerned mainly with ownership of property, while the *Catastro* is concerned mainly with the physical measurements and characteristics. The Property Registry is quite often wrong, so get the catastral certificate and be sure.

If you really have problems with boundaries, it is worth your while to have an official surveyor come and survey the plot. On a transaction of 30 or 40 million pesetas, the 100,000 or so that he charges is very little.

Even those buying apartments will do well to measure their square metres of enclosed space and terraces, to make sure they match the description offered. It is astonishing how often the flat actually has fewer square metres than stated. If you discover this, it may make a bargaining point for getting the price down.

Buyers of rural land will certainly need a property surveyor to measure the land and identify its boundaries. In these cases, even the Catastral department may not have the correct data. Too many rural properties state only that the finca borders on the north with Juan Garcia's farm, and that is simply not good enough.

The contract must also fully identify the seller and buyer.

Remember that the seller is the owner of the property, not the estate agent handling the deal. It is always a bad practice to make your cheque out to an agency. You should know exactly who the seller is and make your cheque directly to him. If the seller insists on anonymity, meaning a bearer cheque, make sure that no money changes hands until you are actually at the Spanish Notary, where you will sign the final contract.

Make your cheques out only to the name of the seller. In the case of reserve deposits before the sale is completed, and where you may never have met the absentee seller, insist that your cheque be deposited in an escrow account, a Bonded Client Account, meaning that the money can be paid out only to the seller and only when the specified time limit has elapsed.

In a few cases, unscrupulous estate agents have taken advantage of distressed or innocent sellers, telling them that they can obtain only a very low price for their property. This might be a widow, who has returned to her home country and wants to sell her Spanish property because she needs the money. The agent tells her he can get only 15 million pesetas for the property. She had the idea it must be worth

20 million or more in today's brisk market, but she lets herself be convinced. The agent also convinces her to sign an agreement which authorises him to keep anything he can get over that price. The agent then sells the property for 25 million pesetas, just as he knew he could, making himself a "commission" of 10 million pesetas. The buyer makes out the cheque to the estate agent, who puts 10 million in his own account and 15 million to the owner. All legal and in order. He never tells the seller what he sold it for, and since the buyer and seller never come into contact, the truth is never discovered. Even if it was, the agent has done nothing illegal. After all, the seller signed the agreement, didn't she? This sort of sharp operating becomes a great temptation for agents where owners are often absentee and ignorant.

Even though the final figure of the purchase price appears on the sales contract, the agent gives the ignorant seller some story about why this had to be done, and, since the agent is acting with a power of attorney to sign the contract for the absentee seller, nothing could be done about it after the fact, in any case.

One extremely important item in your contract is the clause stating the property is sold free of all charges, liens and mortgages. Fine, you say, but how do you really know this is true? This is where your lawyer comes in. He can make a check at the property registry, the *Registro de la Propiedad,* where any such mortgages or liens must be registered against the *escritura*. The *Registro de la Propiedad* is an extremely important office for the property purchaser. Any mortgage on the property must be registered there, and the true owner of the property is listed. For a small fee, the *registro* will give you a *nota simple* for any property. This is a summary of the property's entry into the registry books, which would include a reference to any mortgages pending on the property.

Such a check-up can avoid problems. One horrible case occurred when a British owner returned to Spain to find that his new house had been seized by court order and auctioned off to pay an outstanding mortgage. The locks had been changed and the house, for which he had paid, was no longer his.

His contract did not contain any clause referring to mortgages, so he had no legal remedy at all. If he had such a clause, he could at least have sued the seller for fraud. That is, if he could find him.

And he could have avoided the problem in the first place by having a competent title search made. It is not difficult. A mortgage will be annotated against the property in the Property Registry, even if the seller does not inform you.

He could also have solved the problem if he had been aware that his property was under threat. If he himself had been present in Spain to receive legal notice of the coming seizure and auction, or if he had competent legal representation while he was absent from his property, he could have arranged with the court to pay the mortgage, which attaches to the property itself, not to the previous owner.

Paying the mortgage would have been an unpleasant experience but much cheaper than losing the entire property.

Notices of such legal actions appear by law in the *Boletín Oficial,* the official legal gazette, and often in the local newspapers as well. If the new owner cannot be located by the court, these published notices constitute sufficient legal notice to make the seizure of the property correct in law. Overworked Spanish courts have been severely criticized for failure to make sufficient attempt to locate the absentee owners, but the practice continues.

Furthermore, any legal notification will be sent to the registered owner and mortgage-holder. This means the person who sold you the property, not you. So, you might never find out until too late that the property was being repossessed. It has happened in more than one case.

A lawyer will also check to make sure that no back taxes are owed on the property and that its original registration is in order. Back taxes must be checked with Hacienda or the Town Hall. They are just about the only debts not listed at the Property Registry.

Many more points arise about contracts.

If you are buying a new property which is not yet finished, you can often save money by starting to pay for it early. You want to make sure that your early stage payments do not go directly to the developer, but into an escrow account to which the developer has no access until the flat is finished and delivered to you. Many of today's respectable developers offer this plan.

It prevents the possibility that something goes wrong and the flat is not finished, with you having paid perhaps half its value already. Of course you can sue the developer, but he may have gone broke. Putting the money into these escrow or Bonded Client Accounts also avoids the chance of outright fraud, where a developer simply takes the money and disappears. This sort of fraud was frequent in the 1980's and is rarely seen today but it does happen.

In Seville, for example, 67 Spanish people put down deposits on villas in a new urbanization outside the city, only to discover that the promoters had not even bought the land, let alone begin building the villas. They are suing to recover their money.

So don't start paying for unfinished property without real guarantees, such as the escrow deposit or a bank guarantee, also available, in case the work is not finished.

## Method of Payment

Now you will have to give some thought to your method of payment. One point to consider is whether you are buying from a resident or a non-resident.

Until February 1, 1992, property buyers had to pay Spaniards or residents in pesetas, and had to prove importation of foreign currency if they later wanted to export the money from Spain. With the lifting of exchange controls, this is no longer necessary, although a report must be made to the bank.

You can pay for your Spanish property in pesetas, through a bank cheque, along with a bank certificate that you have imported foreign currency for this purpose, or you can pay by a cheque in foreign currency, or as a non-resident, you can pay by direct transfer from your foreign bank to the seller's foreign bank.

## CERTIFICATE OF NON-RESIDENCE

If you wish to keep the money transfer completely undocumented inside Spain, you can do this, too, but you must then obtain a certificate of non-residence from the Spanish authorities. Be warned that this can take up to two months to obtain, and the Notary will not authorize the completion of the sale without it. If you file your bank certificate and use a normal cheque, this certificate is not necessary.

### Five Per Cent Tax Deposit

*If You Buy from Non-Resident*

Remember also, that if you buy from a non-resident, you must deposit five per cent of the total purchase price with Hacienda in the seller's name, as a guarantee on his taxes.

### Form 211

That is, you pay the seller only 95 per cent of the price. You pay the other five per cent directly to Hacienda, presenting Form 211 to justify your payment.

This amount serves as a guarantee for the non-resident seller's Spanish capital gains tax and for his payment of the annual Spanish wealth tax and non-resident property owner's imputed income tax. Non-resident owners of Spanish property are required to declare two per cent of the official rated value, the *valor catastral,* of their property as if it were income. They then must pay real income tax on this imaginary income. The non-resident pays at a flat rate of 25 per cent. (See section on You and Your Taxes for more details).

If Hacienda discovers that the non-resident seller has failed to keep up his yearly imputed income tax payments, they can retain this amount from the deposit of 5 per cent.

The deposit is mainly designed, however, to cover the non-resident's liability for Spain's capital gains tax of 35 per cent on his profit. As of December 31, 1996, Spain ended the exemption from capital gains for those who owned their property more than 10 years. This was replaced with an inflation correction factor that reduces the capital gains tax but can never eliminate it completely, so most non-resident sellers will be liable for some Spanish capital gains tax. (See Tax section for full details on how this works).

Remember that the *notario* is only there to see that a fair record is kept. Although you may consult the Notary for information, he does not usually act to advise you or the seller, so you need your own legal advice to make sure that your interests are looked after.

Often, the seller of the property will offer to handle all the details for you. This is quite charming of him, but he will put his own interests first.

Let's suppose that all goes well with your checks on the property, and you have signed an *escritura de compraventa,* an official deed of conveyance, at the Notary.

In fact, you no longer sign the contract itself. In these modern times of easy and foolproof copying, the parties to the contract sign a blank sheet of paper, and the Notary keeps these samples in his files for later authentication when necessary. So, nobody can copy your signature from a copy of your title deed because it isn't there.

There still remains one step before the property is offi-cially yours. This is the registry of the deed with the *Registro de la Propiedad*. This registry converts your *escritura de compraventa* into an *escritura pública,* or title deed.

Not until you have your deed registered are you the true owner of the property. In fact, it is the same piece of paper, with a few official stamps on it showing that it has been registered.

The piece of paper itself has no importance. It is the inscription of it in the registry that counts. You yourself will have only a copy of it in any case.

In cases where the same piece of property has been fraudulently sold two or three times, the purchaser who first has it registered will be the owner, regardless of the dates of the other sales.

How do you get the title deed? Once the notary has certified the conveyance deed, you yourself can take the papers directly to the registry office and present it for registry. Or you can have your lawyer do this. Or the developer who is selling the property to you may do it. Or a *gestor* or *administrador de fincas* can do it. Anyone can do it, but somebody has to see that it is done, properly.

In most cases today, you will find that the Notary's office can send a fax immediately upon signing directly to the Property Registry. This notification prevents anyone else from either registering the property or obtaining a mortgage against it instantly, and you are protected until the final registration is done.

Slow as the administrative bureaucracy may be, your deed should be registered within a few months. Usually your lawyer or whoever is handling the matter will ask you for a deposit of money in advance to cover the estimated taxes and fees, and will either bill you for the remainder or refund to you the overpayment when the deed is registered. This is normal and acceptable practice.

If the matter seems to drag on for months, you had better look into what is happening. There was a case a few years ago where one property consultant took people's money, put the cash into his own bank account and the *compraventa* deed into a drawer. He used his clients' money for a year or so, enabling him to make down-payments on Costa del Sol property, and then, at last, presented the deeds for registry. The registry came through in due course and he notified his clients, who often got a small refund, which made them happy. Everyone assumed that it took a year and a half for the registry office to do its work. That is simply not true.

## Property Purchase Checklist

To sum up, you need:

1. Advice from a Spanish lawyer or property consultant.

2. The seller's *escritura publica,* or title deed, as registered in the *Registro de la Propiedad*.

3. A *nota simple* from the Property Registry, showing that no mortgages are registered against the property.

4. A certificate of *Referencia Catastral*. The number itself appears on the IBI receipt, but you want the full certification document that identifies the property.

5. A check on the legality and *plan parcial* if you buy in an urbanization, and assurance of a building permit if you buy a plot.

6. A paid-up receipt for the IBI, *Impuesto sobre Bienes Inmuebles,* or the *declaración de obra nueva*.

7. Receipt for paid-up community charges and a copy of the Statutes if you buy in a condominium.

8. Copies of owner's bills for electricity, water, rubbish collection and even the telephone.

9. A contract, in Spanish, and a translation into your own language, with terms you understand.

10. A decision about your form of payment, whether in pesetas or foreign currency, and be sure to insist on declaring the full amount.

11. An *escritura de compraventa* signed before a *notario*.

12. Payment of fees and taxes, and the five per cent deposit to Hacienda if you buy from a non-resident, using Form 211. Remember the seller is supposed to pay the *plus valía* and the *notario*.

13. An idea of how and when you will get your final *escritura pública,* which makes you the real owner.

## What Can Go Wrong

Let's start with the worst case, a true story: a Danish couple fell in love with a two-bedroom apartment in a still unfinished building right on the sea, just outside Fuengirola on the Costa del Sol. It was perfect for them — not much upkeep, on a quiet stretch of beach but still within strolling distance of town. Work was proceeding on the building while they watched. They had a Spanish lawyer check the contract they were offered. He said it was fine. They signed it, made a fat deposit and returned to Denmark.

Some months later they came back to Spain, expecting to find their retirement home completed. Instead, they found work on the building stopped, a new sign referring to a different building company, and a building guard who said they were not permitted to enter. They were dumbfounded and immediately sought legal advice.

It turned out the man who signed their contracts was not in fact the owner of the building and the developers who employed him had gone bust. The building had a hefty mortgage on it, the bank had repossessed it and auctioned it again to new developers. The new developers were not legally liable to honour the contracts of the earlier developers, as they had nothing to do with them.

The Danish couple discovered that their only recourse was to sue the first developer for the return of their deposit, but they had a hard time finding him and, when they did, he had no money. Four years later, the case was still pending in the backlogged Spanish courts.

This sort of thing does not happen very often. Nor is it only found in Spain. There are fast-moving real estate operators in all countries. The Danish couple did get legal counsel. Their only protection would have been to investigate still more, as a number of lawyers in the area were aware of the doubtful status of the building, and had advised their clients against purchasing there. But not all lawyers were up to date on that particular building.

If the Danish couple had made sure that their deposit was either paid into a Bonded Client Account, an escrow account, or was covered by a bank guarantee in the case of non-completion, they would have been able to recover their money. Be warned, whenever you make a deposit, even on property almost finished.

The advice here is to get as much local information as possible before signing anything. Ask the people who live in the area about a company's reputation, and be wary of unfinished projects. The truth is, nearly all of these projects are completed just as the developer says they will be, but there is always an element of risk.

The case of the Danish couple is extreme. The problems usually encountered are much less serious, though they can be time-consuming and expensive.

## Buying Without *Escritura*

Surprisingly often, the seller does not have an *escritura pública,* for perfectly legitimate reasons, or at least for reasons which will not affect you, the purchaser. Perhaps he has not completed his own purchase yet, or it has taken a longer time than usual. Again, you have to be wary.

One reason for owning property on a private contract only, without a public title deed, is that the property cannot be seized by the court in order to pay a debt of the owner. Only registered property can be attached by a court. Another reason is simply to avoid the payment of the transfer taxes and fees, which can total 10 per cent or even more of the value. A third reason is, of course, to conceal assets, either from a creditor or the tax man, or an ex-wife, for example. When the Property Register is checked, there is nothing listed under that name. On the Spanish Costas, where there was a freewheeling property market for some years, many properties changed hands so quickly as buyers sought quick profits that they simply did not register them. They just waited for the next buyer to carry out all the formalities.

You may find, for example, that a house you fancy has had two or three owners in the last five or six years; that not one of them ever got his final *escritura pública,* or even that the house does not legally exist, as it has never been declared to the tax authorities in a *declaración de obra nueva.* The only legal document for the property simply refers to the plot of land and does not even mention the house.

Or you might be buying a tract of land in the *campo,* the owners of which are seven brothers whose family has never had a written document.

There are perfectly legal ways of solving all these problems. You can have the piece of land made over to you by the original seller, probably the developer of the urbanization, and you yourself can make the *declaración de obra nueva,* even though you did not build the house.

But be careful. If you want to establish the title through a series of private contracts, for example, you may find that you are liable for quite a lot of back taxes, perhaps two or three *plus valías* which have never been paid by the previous owners. Remember, this tax will be charged to the present owner of the property.

## 205 Procedure

One solution for a situation in which the property has no registered title at all is called a 205 procedure, after the number of the regulation which controls it. In this process, you obtain from the Property Registry what is called a "negative certification". This means that the Registry has searched its files and finds no registered owner for the property. Here again you will find the *referencia catastral* useful, because it will have an accurate physical description.

You then request that the property be registered in your name because you have bought it from whoever is the seller, who, in turn, justifies his title by whatever document or evidence he presents. This transaction must be published and posted publicly in case anyone wishes to protest. If no protest is made against your claim, in about a year's time you will get a solid title. If you are going to buy under these conditions, be sure to hold back a percentage of the price until the property is registered in your name. No matter how clear-cut the procedure appears when you start, there is always the possibility of some unknown person coming forward with a claim to the title. There is an element of risk.

## *Expediente de Dominio*

This process, roughly translated as an ownership proceeding, requires more time and expense than the 205 procedure, because it involves more investigation and court action. The *expediente de dominio* can also be used to establish title when the property is in fact registered, but in the name of a person who no longer claims it either because he has sold it to someone on a private contract, who has never registered the sale, or perhaps because the original owner has died. This will take about two years. The claim must be published in the official bulletin and evidence taken in court. Finally, the court will rule on the title and it will be solid. There is always the chance of some nephew who should have inherited the property making a claim of his own against the present purchaser, and the court will decide where the best claim lies.

In any of these procedures to establish title and register the property, be warned that you will be unable to obtain any mortgage funding, and you cannot borrow against the property for two years after its registration.

In any of these cases, you need sound legal advice. Ask around among older residents for an *abogado* or an *administrador de fincas* or a *gestor* whom they can really recommend. You will have to invest a certain amount of your own time and energy in the matter. If you are unable to spend much time in Spain, make sure you have someone you trust look after your affairs in this country. Even your lawyer can put your case on the back burner unless from time to time someone reminds him, in person, that you are concerned. Tax bills and legal notices can come to your address and be ignored if you don't have someone there to check up.

### Property Owned by an Offshore Company

You might also be offered property already owned by an offshore company registered in one of the many "tax havens" around the world.

This means that the property is not registered in the name of the owner. It is registered in the name of a company located in Gibraltar or Panama or the Caiman Islands. The owner in turn owns the company.

These "tax havens" earn their name because they are legal jurisdictions where taxes on locally registered companies are nil or very small, and secrecy is assured from the owner's own tax jurisdiction.

The advantages are clear. When you sell your Spanish property, it is only the company that is transferred. The same company continues to own the same Spanish property, so no Spanish transfer taxes, which can amount to 10 per cent, are charged. Only the offshore company has a new owner. The same applies for inheritance tax when the company is bequeathed to an inheritor. The offshore location charges no tax on this.

The disadvantages are that Spain, keenly aware of the tax loss, has placed a flat tax of three per cent per year on any property held by an offshore company. They have a list of tax havens. European Union authorities are also preparing to place restrictions on these companies, so it is becoming a doubtful proposition.

In the Spanish property boom of the 1980's, these companies became very popular, but they don't look so good now, in most cases, even though they remain perfectly legal. See section on Taxes for more details on offshore companies.

## Bank Repossessions and Auctions

After the 1989 crash of the Spanish property boom, the sunshine coasts were littered with real bargains. Some of these bargains were on sale by people who could not continue the payments on their property, or who needed the cash for other purposes, some of them were offered at cut-rate prices by developers who were stuck with stock they couldn't sell, and some of them were villas and apartments that had been repossessed by banks when their buyers failed to meet the mortgage payments. Bank foreclosure of mortgages is one of the few Spanish legal procedures that works quickly and effectively. A few of the properties were even those seized by courts and sold at auction to satisfy a debt against the owner, as in several of the frightening examples we have seen earlier in this section.

The standard wisdom today, in the new millennium, is that all of these bargain properties have been sold, and the few remaining are those which are so undesirable that nobody wants them at any price. This is mainly true, but there are still some real bargains available if you look for them.

This means time and effort on your part, but it can be well worth your while.

One of the easiest ways to make a stab at buying a cut-price property is simply to walk into the offices of bank managers in an area where you would like to live. Go into the bank, say that you would like to speak with the manager about a business matter. He will probably speak English and he will probably receive you after a short wait. Say to him, "I am interested in buying a repossessed property. *Reposesión*. Do you have any on your books?

You may be as astonished as I was when he points to a stack of *escrituras* on his desk and says, "How about one of these?" If the bank is a bit more modern, he may punch up a list on his computer terminal and inquire about the price range that interests you. So, you look at the list and pick a villa or an apartment that seems promising. You view it, like it, and buy it from the bank for maybe half what it would fetch on the market. It can be that easy.

So why aren't these properties already sold, you ask. Good question. The answer seems to be that banks simply don't know how to sell real estate. A few of them have established their own departments for selling their repossessed properties, but most of them just sit in the files until the court gets around to auctioning them off at official proceedings.

So, although the conventional wisdom is largely correct, more than a few decent properties still remain with the banks. If you are willing to make an effort to search them out, some great bargains are waiting for you.

Be prepared to haggle with the bank and be sure to have your lawyer help you. If the bank says they will take 20 million for the property you are told is worth 25 million, offer them 15. Keep in mind that the next bank will also have some repossessions available.

If you really feel like getting into the system, you could even try the court-ordered auctions of property being sold to satisfy debts. These auctions, called *subastas,* can offer some incredible bargains to those who get into the know on how they work. Properties have been sold at one-tenth their real value, for example. Yes, in northern European countries this simply cannot take place, but under the Spanish system the court is obliged to take the highest offer, no matter how low, after the property has been offered several times.

And, yes, you are right if you think that this system attracts abuses. In many courts, there are professional *subasteros* who work together, sometimes in collusion with corrupt court officials, to offer low bids. Later, these professionals split the take among themselves. They often assign the properties to third parties, who are not real buyers, but who also get their share of the profits once the property is sold on again.

## Auctions:

### *A Worst-Case Scenario*

### *A Spanish man owns half my house because of an embargo I didn't even know existed. What can I do?*

IN AUGUST, 1992, I bought a house on the Costa Blanca, through a contract drawn up by a Spanish lawyer. I then returned to Sweden, where I received instructions from the lawyer on how to make up a Power of Attorney - a *poder* - which authorised the lawyer to act for me in the sale. I sent this Power of Attorney to my lawyer in Spain.

The following series of events took place. Perhaps the chronology is important.

**August, 1992** - Private contract drawn up by Spanish lawyer.

**September, 1992** - Power of Attorney made up.

**January, 1993** - From Stockholm I contact my lawyer about the final sales contract. I and the seller, a widowed Scandinavian woman, each sign the contract, and I send my lawyer, by fax, a copy of the statement of full payment, so that he can sign for me the *escritura de compraventa*, the official title contract, at the Spanish notary's office.

**February, 1993** - I receive in Sweden a fax for the notarial fee and the lawyer's fee for handling the transaction

**March, 1993** - I return to Spain, and pay the fees. All seems to be in good order and I receive my copy of the *escritura*, the title for the house. That is, until:

**May, 1996** - A Spanish woman whom I do not know calls at my house in Spain, telling me there is an "embargo" on the house, dated September, 1992, as a result of an unpaid bill from a carpentry shop, charged to the dead husband of the widow who sold me the house.

The husband had died in December of 1991, and the "embargo" for his debt was levied on his half of the house, as both husband and wife had their names on the title deed.

I tried to talk with my Spanish lawyer, whom I found to be very busy now. He left a message via his secretary that the "embargo" was nothing to worry about, that it was against the previous owner of the house, and, as he was deceased, the "embargo" would disappear without my doing anything. I also wrote to my lawyer in Sweden, to send a letter to the woman who sold me the house, demanding that she pay the carpentry bill and settle the "embargo".

**August, 1996** - I receive in my post box a notification to the deceased husband of the widow who sold me the house, to come to the court in Alfaz del Pi. I go to the court myself, where I find out the name of the lawyer acting for the layers of the "embargo". Yes, the reason for the charge against the property is the unpaid bill from the carpenter shop, for the supply of doors and frames.

**September, 1996** - I try to contact this lawyer but I am never able to speak to him in person. My Spanish is not very good but I try to explain to the lawyer's secretary that I want the layer of the "embargo" to contact me directly, as I am unable to find the exact address of this carpenter shop. The carpenter never contacts me. As my own lawyer had told me in his message that the charge would eventually be dropped without my doing anything, I took this non-contact as assurance that the problem was not urgent.

**October, 1997** - I received a certified letter, addressed to myself this time, asking me to come to a Spanish Notary in Benidorm. There I met a local man and his lawyer, who, to my astonishment, told me that half of my house (the half of the title that belonged to the deceased husband), had been sold to this man at an official court auction, and he is now the legal owner of half of the property.

My new lawyer has spoken with this man's lawyer. They offer to sell me the man's share for 12 million pesetas, so I can own all of my house. My new lawyer also found out that this man bought the half share of the property for 1.2 million pesetas, one-tenth of what he is asking for it!

How can this be?

- Since I moved to Spain in March of 1993, I received no letter, reminder, or notification, except as noted here.
- An unpaid bill from a carpenter shop has turned into half the value of my house.
- I have an *Escritura*, or title deed, which shows that there are no debts, embargoes or mortgages on the property.

The real value of the house on the market today is between 30 and 35 million pesetas. When the "embargo" was placed in September of 1992, the value was estimated at seven million pesetas, keeping in mind that construction of the house was not completely finished at that time. Since then, I have spent a lot of money to finish the house.

I do not trust Spanish lawyers any more. Are there any cases similar to mine? What can be done to solve my problem?

-P.O. (Alfaz del Pi)

YES, UNFORTUNATELY, THERE ARE a number of cases similar to yours. They are also similar in that they have no easy solutions.

In Malaga, 67 families, most of them Germans, must either pay outstanding mortgages against their holiday flats, of which they were not informed when they bought, or lose their properties.

How can this be, you ask. In the case of the German families, it was direct fraud and it happened like this:

The flats were of new construction. It is quite common for builders to obtain mortgages from banks when the property is well under construction in order to get cash to finish the project. These mortgages are themselves also registered in the Property Registry as a lien against the property.

Normally, the buyer or his lawyer checks the Property Registry when preparing the purchase. You ask for a *nota simple*, a simple note, which gives the details of the registration, and, just as importantly, includes a reference to any charges registered against it. This is how you find out if there is a mortgage or a lien against the property before you buy.

In most cases, the builder pays off the mortgage and has the note removed when he sells the flat, thus delivering a clear title, free of charges or liens. Anybody who buys a new property should make this check. It is basic practice.

However, in the case of the German buyers, the property developer committed a direct fraud. There is always a brief interval between the time the Property Registry is checked for mortgages or liens and the signing of the sales contract and its subsequent inscription in the Registry in the name of the new owner.

During this time, the properties remain officially registered in the name of the seller. Our larcenous developer here, immediately after his German buyers had checked the Registry, but before they had finalized their purchases, took out a bank mortgage against each of the properties. The innocent buyers had their *nota simple*, showing that

53

no mortgages existed, so they went ahead and signed their purchase contracts and then had the contracts inscribed in the Property Registry as *escritura publica*. No one told them that a mortgage now existed against their titles, and they did not discover this until more than a year later when the bank began repossession actions against the properties because the mortgage had never been paid.

The Germans must either pay off the mortgages, amounting to about five million pesetas per flat, or lose their properties to the bank because the bank acted in perfect good faith, has an officially registered lien on the property, and its mortgage payments are a preferential debt in law. The only comeback for the defrauded purchasers is a lawsuit against the promoter, who has been sentenced to six years in jail for fraud. Unfortunately, he has no assets to pay back the money.

This is a case similar to yours, where direct fraud is involved. I hope this gives you an idea of the hole in the Spanish property registration system which allows such a fraud to be committed. At least the German purchasers found out about the mortgages before their properties had been auctioned off to pay the debt.

Why weren't they informed, you now ask. Good question. All official court and bank notifications were, of course, directed to the officially registered owner of the properties at the time of taking out the mortgage. That is to say, the property developer and holder of the mortgages. The new owners did not figure in the case, so they were not notified.

This would also be your own case. All court proceedings took place between the layer of the lien, the carpentry shop, and the debtor, or his estate, if the debtor was deceased. That is why you received an official notification to the dead husband to present himself at the court in Alfaz del Pi. As far as the court was concerned, you yourself did not even exist.

In your own case, there does not appear to be any fraudulent intent, but rather an unfortunate series of coincidences, or perhaps a lack of due care in the purchase, complicated by the loophole in the Spanish registration system. Neither does there appear to be any magic bullet which will easily solve your problem. The case is complex and we hope your new lawyer is strongly motivated to dig into it.

Let's take a look at the facts we have.

At some point, the deceased husband ordered material from the carpentry. He did not pay for it. The carpentry obtained from the court a lien against the man's property to satisfy the unpaid debt. The man's property in Spain consisted of half-ownership of the house.

Let's use the term "lien", which is the correct English legal term, instead of the Spanish term "embargo" to describe this charge. English speakers have come to accept the direct translation as "embargo" but it is not the correct term in English.

The court orders this lien registered in the *Registro de la Propiedad* against the property. This means that, if the debt is not paid, the court will order the property sold at public auction to obtain money for the creditor. The lien attaches to the property, not to the person. Thus, if the property passes by inheritance, the lien goes with it. If the property is sold, the lien goes with it, as you have sadly discovered.

**Many Abuses Occur In Public Auctions**

Finally, as the debt was not paid, the property was sold at auction. All notifications would have been sent to the registered property owner at the time of the lien, that is, the deceased husband. If no one was present to receive these in Spain, the notice of auction is published in the official Bulletin of the province, and posted in the municipality, and the auction can legally proceed. In the case of the death of the debtor and the absence of the widow, we can see how notification never reached you, the eventual buyer.

In most northern European countries, there is a series of protections for people who have their property seized by the court and sold at auction. These protections include the regulation that the property must be sold at something near its market value and that any money left after paying the debt must be paid to the person who has lost his property.

In theory, similar protections exist in Spain, but they are routinely ignored. In addition, court-ordered auctions, or *subastas*, are subject to many abuses in practice. Sometimes professional *subasteros* will work together, perhaps even with corrupt court officials, to make sure that only the lowest bids are presented. In a recent case in Madrid, 17 people face criminal charges for this practice. In the end, the court has no option but to accept the low bids.

Even without supposing corruption or collusion in your own case, those who are in the know about auctions can, perfectly legally, take advantage of the opportunity to buy property cheaply. You can do this yourself by familiarizing yourself with the court bulletin board and reading the official publications.

So this is how your 1.2 million peseta debt was settled. And the buyer got himself a half-interest in a property worth perhaps 30 million pesetas. Pretty tempting.

Now, there is almost certainly nothing that can be done to protest the auction. The court ordered it and we can be quite sure that all the formalities were correctly observed. Unless your lawyer can find evidence of some criminal action, the matter is finished at that level.

At last we come to some possible courses of action for you, none of them easy.

You can proceed against the widow, the seller of the property. It will help if you can establish some responsibility on her part to deceive you.

Or you can proceed against your own lawyer at that time, if you can show that he was negligent in failing to discover any charges against the property.

First, we suppose that your purchase contract contains a clause stating that the property is sold free of charges, liens and encumbrances. On the face of it, your seller should have known that there was a charge against the property and so she acted fraudulently in selling to you. Even if she didn't know, she ought to have known, and so she is in violation of the contract.

As a note, it is perfectly possible that she didn't know about the lien. Yes, as you say in the beginning, the chronology is important. If we suppose that she inherited the deceased husband's half of the property before August, 1992, enabling her to sell to you the entire house, she may never have checked the registry to discover that she had also inherited a lien on the debt.

Then, let's see if your original lawyer did his job correctly. If you signed a private contract to purchase the house in August of 1992, and your lawyer acted immediately to check the Property Registry, he would have found that no liens or mortgages were inscribed against the house.

Do you in fact have in your purchase files a copy of this *nota simple*? No lawyer would advise on a purchase without one.

Supposing your efficient lawyer had done this before the end of August, we then see that the lien was registered in September of 1992, without you or your lawyer knowing about it.

Then in January of 1993 you complete the purchase, with an official contract made before the Spanish notary, and, I suppose, being registered in the Property Registry. In the Registry there is also a note of the lien against half of the property. This lien has now passed once by inheritance and once by purchase, without anyone knowing about it.

Should your lawyer, as a matter of prudence, have checked the Property Registry again in January of 1993, as so much time had passed since August of 1992? This may be an important question, if you choose to act against him for professional negligence. If you do take this course, be assured that all Spanish lawyers are obliged to carry a professional indemnity insurance, which varies from province to province, but usually values around 100 million pesetas.

On the basis of the facts presented here, these two possibilities seem the only courses available to you and your new Spanish lawyer will be in the best position to advise you.

Other purchasers of Spanish property should be advised to close this loophole of ownership by obtaining a note from the Property Registry immediately before their contract is signed at the Spanish notary and making sure that the notarized contract is inscribed in the Property Registry immediately after the signing.

The Notary can even send a fax immediately to the Property Registry, advising that the contract is signed, which will prevent any mortgage or charge from being registered until the contract is physically delivered to the Registry.

## Buyer, Be Warned
### *You Will Pay Capital Gains Tax*

Although we have mentioned before that most of today's purchasers on the Spanish Costas and islands are buying property in the sun in order to enjoy it, rather than as speculators who intend to sell it for profit, any property purchaser likes to think that, if he sells his flat or villa, he can make some profit.

Prices are indeed rising and demand is brisk. But today's buyers need to be warned Spain has already removed an important deduction from its system of capital gains tax.

The reduction factor of 11.11 per cent per year for each year you have owned your property, starting after the first two years, with no capital gains tax at all after 10 years of ownership, ended as of December 31, 1996.

Sellers of property, or any other assets, acquired after that date, can now apply only a coefficient of reduction that more or less matches the inflation rate, meaning that your Spanish property purchase will certainly attract capital gains tax when you sell it on after some years.

Those property sellers who speak glowingly of profits to be made in a few years usually forget to mention this point.

(See section on "You and Your Taxes" for more complete information about your capital gains tax and your annual Spanish wealth tax and naming a fiscal representative.)

## Spain Passes Timeshare Law

On January 5, 1999, more than a year and a half after the "final" deadline, Spain's timeshare law at last went into effect. The law regulates important legal aspects of timeshare itself and provides consumer protection that brings the country into line with European timeshare regulations.

Putting a crimp into the high-pressure selling techniques of the timeshare touts around bus stations and tourist spots, the law provides a 10-day cooling-off period during which no deposit may be taken and the buyer can withdraw from the contract he has signed without any penalty.

Furthermore, the law requires that the timeshare operator provide full information and a contract in the buyer's own language. If any element of the purchase does not meet the brochure or written description or match the contract terms, the buyer has a further three months to rescind the contract unilaterally with no penalty.

The law also provides that any loan which the buyer may have taken out to purchase the timeshare will also be cancelled. This has been one tricky aspect of hard sales, in which the timeshare seller offers a low-interest loan to the prospective buyer. All well and good, but if the buyer later wants out of his contract, he finds that he still owes the loan to the bank, a third party, and it must be paid off. This practice is ended by the new law.

The law also provides that all contracts will be subject to Spanish law. That is, even if the buyer's contract states that its terms are subject to the laws of some distant offshore jurisdiction, where the timeshare company's headquarters is located, this provision is not valid and the contract will be subject to interpretation in Spanish courts.

This has been a thorny point in many timeshare contracts because the buyers found it difficult to dispute any point when the court was thousands of miles away.

Even the service companies which maintain the resorts in good condition have, until now, often been registered in offshore tax havens.

This made it difficult for timeshare buyers to bring action against the companies when they failed to keep the resorts in good condition.

Under terms of Spain's new law, the service companies must have a permanent establishment registered inside Spain, where they can be held legally responsible.

Furthermore, the new law makes the resort owner finally responsible for proper maintenance of the resort, and action can be taken against the resort owner if the service company fails to perform.

On the other hand, the resort operator can repossess an owner's holiday weeks if the owner fails to pay one year's maintenance charges. The operator must give 30 days certified notice before he can do this, and, unless this right is specifically renounced in your contract, he must pay back the owner the value of his remaining weeks in the scheme.

That is, a timeshare plan may run from a minimum of three years to a maximum of 50 years. If an owner has used his weeks for 25 years in a 50-year plan, and then defaults, the operator must him back half of his original price, as well as assuming the debt owed by the owner to the service company.

However, it is also possible for the timeshare contract to contain a penalty clause which will let the company keep the entire amount originally paid. Watch out for this clause in your timeshare contract.

The law also provides that timeshare contracts can be registered in Spain's Property Registry as a special right, although the law is also very careful to note that timeshare is not a property right as such, that it is a service contract not a property sale.

The full name of the law in fact is The Law Regulating the Rights of Rotational Enjoyment of Real Estate for Touristic Use, and it forbids any mention of property rights in timeshare publicity.

Spain's law also provides a stunning innovation: a tax on timeshare sales. Can you believe that a business which has

500,000 owners in Spain and which generated sales of 97,500 million pesetas in 1998 alone has never had its sales taxed?

Spain will now tax all timeshare sales at 7 per cent, the reduced VAT rate.

Imagine if this tax had been applied over the last 20 years, during which about two billion pounds of timeshare was sold in Spain. That 140 million pounds would have helped the Spanish Social Security system cut the medical waiting lists by quite a lot.

## Expropriation of Property

For most people, any improvement of the road system or flyovers and bypasses to increase safety is good news. But it may not be such good news if your property borders a projected highway or is affected by a new bypass, because the authorities — represented by a public works department such as the *Ministerio de Obras Públicas y Transportes* or MOPT — can expropriate your property and put you off it. They must pay you, of course, and here the doctrine of *justiprecio* applies, meaning they must pay you a fair price. You may have to fight them to get it, however.

There are legal avenues open to you to protect your rights in the matter.

First, the authorities must officially inform you that expropriation proceedings are about to begin against you. They will send you an official letter inviting you to attend the *acta previa a la ocupación*. This is a hearing, usually held in your town hall, at which you may present any protest you have about the extent of your property being expropriated.

Money is not discussed at this first hearing, only the amount of land being taken. You should take skilled legal counsel with you when you go to this hearing.

If the authorities are only interested in a few square metres of your vast finca, then you have no real problem. If, however, they want to put the road through the kitchen and reception area of your popular restaurant, or if the amount of land they take will leave you with too few square metres to be buildable, then there must be some negotiating.

These are two typical, worst-case situations, which occur with some frequency. In this case, some lawyers advise that you attempt to make the authorities expropriate your *entire* property and not just part of it. This obviously is because the property, once divided, becomes all but worthless and such a situation is manifestly unfair to the person involved.

In these negotiations, the authorities are usually reasonable and fair, but they will be even more fair and reasonable when confronted by skilled counsel.

Your chances of resisting expropriation altogether are very poor indeed. The entire concept of expropriation or Eminent Domain exists because sometimes the public good takes precedence over private ownership. They are going to build the highway and your chance of moving the route away from your private property is very small.

Once the amount of land being expropriated is agreed, the authorities take the situation under analysis and then communicate their offer of payment to each owner. If the offer is acceptable, you inform them and the deal is done.

If, however, as is more frequent, you are not satisfied with their offer, you negotiate again. The doctrine of *justiprecio* is not just a word and it can be enforced. You will need to prepare a case for a higher price on your property, including sales prices of land around you, improvements you have made, and so on. You will need expert advice for this.

If you are unable to come to an agreement with the authorities by negotiation, you have recourse to the *Jurado de Expropiaciones,* which is a special court set up for this purpose only. The presiding members of this tribunal are not only judges; real estate experts are also included, and decisions it has rendered have ensured that fair market value is paid to many owners.

Beyond that, you can appeal this tribunal's ruling to the normal courts all the way up to the Supreme Court.

To sum up, in any expropriation proceedings, you have little chance of resisting entirely the order. But you do have two opportunities to protest both the amount of land being taken and the payment offered. Skilled counsel can make sure your interests are protected.

## Financing Your Spanish Property

There are a number of ways in which you can finance your Spanish property over periods up to 15 years, just as you probably did when you first purchased a house in your own country. Mortgages of 20 and 30 years, however, are only beginning to make their appearance in Spain.

### *Financing by the developer*

Let's look first at financing which may be offered you by the developer of the project where you purchase. There are dozens of different schemes here and you should be wary.

The contract must stipulate the down payment, enumerate the following payments and state when such payments end. It will be clear from the total of these payments just how much the developer's financing will cost you in comparison to paying cash. If the difference is acceptable to you, then you have a deal.

Make sure you know what happens if you miss a payment. There should be some provision which is not too harmful to you, allowing you to make a certain number of late payments for only a small penalty.

Another essential provision will allow you to pay off the remainder of the contract in a lump sum at any time you choose, without having to pay the total remaining interest. You might at a future date come into money, enabling you to make such a payment, or your own currency may fluctuate enough against the peseta to make such payment favourable to you at a time when the value of your own currency is high. Or, you may wish to pay off your terms with the developer in order to resell the property.

Developers often offer excellent terms to purchasers who begin their payments before the building is finished. This can be favourable to the buyer, but he must be sure that the developer is reliable and solvent, and can bring the project to completion.

Often, the developer offers a bank guarantee which assures the buyer the return of his invested money if the project stalls or fails. An important point is that this bank guarantee will cost the buyer a small percentage of the price. It is a separate transaction with the bank, not necessarily included in all contracts. If the developer offers this guarantee, details must be clearly spelled out, either in the contract or in a separate document.

Finally, Spanish consumer legislation passed in 1996 requires that all contracts spell out terms clearly. Do not be afraid to ask plenty of questions.

Yes, we recommend that you use a Spanish lawyer, under *all* circumstances. Follow the old legal axiom: the seller may not need a lawyer, but the buyer always does.

## Bank Loans and Mortgages

With the lifting of almost all exchange controls, both residents and non-residents may now obtain loans and mortgages against their Spanish property in any currency from any bank in the world — if they can find a bank willing to lend against property in another country. Even very long-term endowment mortgages are beginning to appear, offered by Spanish branches of UK lending institutions.

The good news is the inflation and interest rates are at an all-time low in Spain, with a prime lending rate of only 5.25 per cent. Spanish bank mortgages are now being offered at rates of less than seven per cent, the lowest in Europe, but the percentages fluctuate quite often.

Those people purchasing a second home in Spain may find they can obtain a mortgage in their home country for the purchase of property in Spain. This could represent an ideal solution, but UK residents in particular must be careful about losing MIRA tax relief on their UK tax when they mortgage to purchase property outside the UK, and they will have to pay UK tax on their loan repayments to the

Spanish bank should they mortgage in Spain because the Spanish lending bank will not pay these taxes.

For non-UK foreigners in Spain, the introduction of the Euro means that, as of January 1, 1999, mortgages can be denominated in Euros, at interest rates controlled by the European Central Bank. The Spanish base rate, known as the Mibor, or Madrid rate, will also apply for some mortgages for a time as yet not determined. One of the principal advantages of the Euro-mortgage is that holders will not have to worry about currency fluctuations and exchange rates.

## Subsidized Housing

In Spain, as in most countries, the government subsidizes some types of housing. Ordinarily, this housing is destined for the poor and is offered to them on favourable terms.

Such housing is known in Spain as V.P.O., or *Vivienda de Protección Oficial*. You may think that this housing is not meant to help well-to-do foreigners purchase vacation homes, and you would be right. But there are several classes of V.P.O. projects. One class, operated by the Spanish government, is available only to the poor, who must make a declaration of poverty in order to obtain it.

The other class, more frequently seen, is based on the provision of cheap government financing to the project developer, and these apartments are available to foreigners, although controls are becoming stricter. Purchasers now must be residents and they cannot have incomes of more than about 250,000 pesetas a month.

Nevertheless, especially if you are an official resident of Spain, earning a living here, with a modest income, you may qualify for government assistance in buying your home, just as Spaniards do.

Remember, when purchasing V.P.O. flats, the offer will stipulate that you make a small down payment, but if you can make a larger payment (two to three million pesetas) and thus totally clear the constructor's own financial contribution to the project, this will be very advantageous. The balance, payable over 15 years or more on favourable terms, will then repay only the cheap government loan and not contribute further to the constructor's profit.

There are, of course, controls on the resale of such flats, which block speculators profiting at the expense of the government.

## Insuring Your Home

As in any country, it is sound practice to carry homeowners insurance protecting you against damage to the building itself, damage or theft of its contents, and against claims from others who may suffer injury or damage resulting from your ownership.

This is especially important when you are absent from your Spanish property for long periods, but be alert to clauses in your contract which render your insurance invalid if you are away from the property for more than a stated period of time. Often, by paying an extra premium, you can be covered even though you are absent much of the time.

Both Spanish and international insurers offer various policies at various prices. Make enquiries among older residents to find a company which has given good service.

As in most countries, you fill out a form in which you put a value you wish to insure on your house and its contents. Remember that, should you choose to insure your property for only half its real value, the insurance company, which makes its own evaluation, will pay you only half the value of any individual items which are stolen or damaged. People sometimes think they can insure half and then get full value when only two or three items are stolen or damaged, but this is not so.

The company will also ask you to report on whether your property will be unoccupied for lengthy periods, how old the building is, how many doors and windows there are, whether they are guarded by iron-barred *rejas,* if there is a burglar alarm system, and so on. If you do not respond truthfully to these questions, there can be grounds for a later denial of any claim you make. Your premiums will vary according to your situation.

Be sure to read the fine print in your policy. Often, insurance against theft of the contents of your property will not pay unless entrance has been forced and there is evidence for this. If a "guest" at one of your parties makes off with your wife's jewels, you will not be paid. If there is no copy of the contract available in your language, have someone translate for you.

What will insurance cost you? Policies and conditions vary, but you can estimate that about 1,000 pesetas per year per million pesetas of value will cover the building itself against damage by natural causes or fire or explosions, if the building is located in a town. An older house in the country, far from fire-fighting services, would cost more to insure.

Insurance of your furniture and household effects will be somewhere around 2,500 pesetas per million of value if you live in an apartment; up to 3,500 pesetas per million if you live in a detached villa. This covers fire and theft.

If one of your steps collapses and the postman breaks his leg, or you leave the bathtub water running until your downstairs neighbour's apartment is flooded, they can claim compensation from you as the owner. You can cover yourself for claims up to 10 million pesetas for less than 2,500 pesetas a year.

Most Spanish companies offer a comprehensive policy covering the building, the contents and third party claims. In addition, if you live in an apartment, you may find that your Community of Owners carries a general policy on the entire building or row of houses.

# CONTENTS

CHAPTER TWO

# Selling

## Seller, Beware!

### *It's Not Only Buyers Who Find Traps In Property Sales*

So, you want to sell your Spanish property. Maybe you are getting very old and want to spend your last days in your home country. Maybe you want to move to a smaller place, or a bigger place. Maybe you think you can make a profit.

In any of these cases, there is good news and bad news for prospective sellers of Spanish property. First, the good news.

A weak peseta means that foreign buyers, especially the British, are getting more value for their pounds, marks or dollars, so the property market is moving briskly. The British in particular have returned to buy homes in the Spanish sun. Germans are buying, too.

Second, reduction factors were applied to Spanish capital gains tax and the liability for the tax itself was limited in time. Until December 31, 1996, Spanish property owners could deduct 11.11 per cent per year from their profits, and paid no capital gains tax at all after 10 years of ownership. Many sellers today will still benefit from these reductions. If you bought before 1987, meaning that you have owned your property for 10 years before the December 31, 1996, cut-off date, you will have no capital gains tax at all.

Furthermore, property prices on the Spanish coasts and islands have been reaching boom levels in the last few years, rising at more than 20 per cent in the hottest second-home areas in 1999. Experts predict the rate to slow somewhat for the year 2000, although they also predict that prices will continue to rise.

The bad news is that a sale of Spanish property will attract transfer costs that can total as much as 20 per cent of the price, in addition to that capital gains tax.

In some areas, real estate agents charge commissions of 10 per cent. Add to this taxes and costs that total about 10 per cent and you are looking at some very high transfer costs.

## Taxation Laws
*Stricter Today*

Furthermore, today's property sellers face a much more strictly applied set of tax regulations. In the bad old days, both private sellers and developers in Spain often took the money and ran, leaving all transfer costs for the buyer and conveniently "forgetting" that, as sellers, they had Spanish capital gains tax to pay on any profits they had made.

Capital gains tax for non-residents is charged at 35 per cent of the profit, while capital gains tax for residents is limited to 20 per cent of the profit. For those who bought their Spanish property before 1994, reductions are available. After the first two years of ownership, you can deduct 11.11 per cent per year from your profits. After 10 years of ownership, there is no capital gains tax. But the end of 1996, remember, is now the cutoff point for this reduction. Hence, no reduction at all is available for those who bought in 1995, because the two-year period runs into the cutoff date.

This capital gains tax is charged on profit, remember. That is the difference between your original purchase cost of the property and the price at which you sell it today. If you bought for 15 million and you sell for 21 million, you have a profit of 6 million pesetas.

Let's say you bought your holiday flat in the boom year of 1989. So, you owned the property for seven years before Dec. 31, 1996.

You fall into the transitional period that runs across both systems of capital gains tax, before Dec. 31, 1996, and after that date.

So you get to apply a bit of both systems.

(See Section on Taxes for a complete picture of capital gains tax).

First, you can apply a multiplying factor of 1.02 to your original purchase price, thus increasing it by 300,000 pesetas, which makes your profit only 5.7 million. This is called the *coeficiente de actualización,* the factor that brings your original purchase price into line with today's inflated pesetas.

In your case, the factor does not make up completely for the inflation since 1989, because the government knows that you also have a piece of the 11.11 per cent per year reduction factor.

If you have owned the property for seven years before the end of 1996, you subtract the first two years, leaving five years of reductions of 11.11 per cent. That gives you 55.55 per cent reduction. Rounding off the numbers, you are looking at a tax base of 2.5 million pesetas, half of the profit you started with.

If you are a non-resident, your capital gains tax rate is 35 per cent. Applied to 2.5 million pesetas, this gives about 850,000 pesetas in tax which you owe to Spain's Hacienda.

Spain ensures that the non-resident seller will pay this tax and cannot simply leave the country with the money by the following procedure:

The buyer himself must pay a deposit of five per cent of the total purchase price directly to Hacienda when he purchases from a non-resident. This means that the non-resident seller receives only 95 per cent of the price. If the seller chooses to disappear, the Spanish tax man does not lose. Five per cent of his total purchase price is being held by Hacienda.

In practice, this five per cent turns out to be close to his real capital gains tax in most cases. In the example cited above, a sale of 20 million pesetas, we find that five per cent comes to one million pesetas. The non-resident capital gains tax was 850,000 pesetas, so our seller still owes another 150,000 pesetas to Hacienda. He must declare and pay this within 30 days after the sale on Form 212.

However, our seller in the example made quite a good profit, realizing a gain of 35 per cent in his seven years of ownership. Most sellers make a smaller profit, meaning that their real tax due is smaller than the five per cent of the total price already held by Hacienda.

The few speculators who have bought beachfront property in Marbella, for example, and have made 50 per cent or even more on their money in two years, will indeed face some stiff capital gains tax.

If you haven't made that much, you can claim back any overpayment from Hacienda.

## File Immediately

*To Claim Overpayment*

For example, supposing that Hacienda has a deposit of 750,000 pesetas on your sale, but your capital gains tax comes to only 400,000 pesetas. Don't worry. You have your lawyer or tax consultant file Form 212 immediately after the sale to claim your overpayment back from the authorities. This is routinely done, although it can take up to six months before you receive your money back. In some cases it has taken more than a year but Hacienda seems to be moving a little faster.

Keep in mind that the deposit is also used as a guaranty against any unpaid non-resident property owner's imputed income tax and wealth tax, as well. So, if you have not paid these taxes for a few years, don't be surprised when Hacienda withholds the amounts due from the deposit on your property sale. After all, if you had a flat valued at 10 million pesetas, this would attract income and wealth tax totalling 70,000 pesetas a year. (See You and Your Taxes for more details). If you had not paid this for four years, you would owe the tax agency 280,000 pesetas, which Hacienda would never see if you simply took the money and returned to your home country.

And, of course, you cannot complete your sale unless you present your paid-up tax forms for the two charges of the current year when you sign the final contract before the Spanish notary.

## Resident Capital Gains
### *Tax Limited to 20%*

If you are a resident, your capital gains tax will not require any deposit from the buyer, whether he is a non-resident or a resident. Your capital gains tax will be calculated as part of your regular Spanish income tax declaration, made from May 1 to June 20 of the year following your sale.

The tax will first be calculated at the same rate as you pay your regular income tax, meaning that, if your regular income is about three million pesetas a year and you are making a joint declaration, you will pay at about 15 per cent because that is your regular Spanish income tax rate. Applied to that same 2.5 million pesetas of taxable profit, you get a tax of a little more than 400,000 pesetas, much better than the non-resident.

If you had a higher income, hence paid Spanish income tax at a higher rate, you would pay your capital gains tax at the same higher rate.

However, the resident's capital gains tax has a top limit of 20 per cent, so you would never pay more than 500,000 pesetas on the 2.5 million taxable profit, no matter how high your income. This is better than the non-resident rate of 35 per cent, which drew tax of 850,000 pesetas.

## Over 65's Free of Capital Gains

New for the year 2000 is the provision that a resident over 65 is exempt from capital tax on their principal residence.

In addition, the resident can be entirely free of capital gains tax if he uses the full amount of his sale to purchase a new principal residence in Spain. That is, if you bought for 10 million pesetas and sold for 15 million pesetas, and you purchase a new Spanish home for 15 million pesetas, thus putting all of the proceeds of your sale back into your residence, you will have no capital gains tax to pay.

If you buy a new principal residence that costs less than the total amount of your sale, you will be able to deduct only a percentage of the amount reinvested.

That is, if you spent 10 million pesetas of your sale proceeds on a new flat, you could deduct only two-thirds of your profit, comparing 10 million to your total take of 15 million in order to get that percentage.

You have three years to carry out this operation. A holiday home does not count for this offset. It must be your new principal residence.

Be warned. You must not purchase your new home before you sell the old one. You must buy it after you sell your original home. Otherwise, you are the owner of two houses and you are selling one of them. When you move to the other, it may not count as a valid offset on your capital gains tax unless you make a specific declaration to this effect when you buy the property. Consult with your tax adviser beforehand.

The non-resident, however, does not have this offset provision, so he must pay the 35 per cent non-resident capital gains tax. By definition, he cannot have his principal residence in Spain if he is not a resident. Furthermore, since the ending of the 10-year limit, he will certainly have some tax to pay and from now on, all non-resident sellers will be subject to the 5 per cent deposit.

## Inflation Correction Factor
### *Is New for Capital Gains*

The old reduction factor of 11.11 per cent per year off profits from a property sale has been replaced, since December 31, 1996, by an inflation correction factor called the *coeficiente de actualización*. You multiply your original purchase price by this factor in order to bring it up to date in today's inflated pesetas, thus reducing your profit, and your capital gains tax.

Neither residents nor non-residents should be too upset by the change. The factor itself is not as favourable to the seller as the old system, but neither is it much worse. The really bad news for sellers is that they will now never, ever, be exempt from capital gains tax, and they will always be subject to the deposit of five per cent if they are non-residents. See the Section on Taxes for a detailed explanation.

## Property Seller's Checklist

### 1. ESTATE AGENT

One rule often cited by those who have sold their homes in Spain is: Don't try to do it yourself. Get an estate agent, or several, and let them handle the showing of the place and dealing with prospects. Otherwise, you go crazy. There may be exceptions to this rule, but most sellers are in agreement.

Very seldom do Spanish estate agents demand the exclusive right to market your property, so you will probably list your sale with several agents in your area. Each agent will have his own form of agreement with you, in which his commission is stated if he brings the client who eventually buys your property. This agreement will contain the commission charged. Some agents charge as high as 10 per cent. Five per cent is more frequent. You make your own deal on this.

An agent can be very helpful to you in decisions such as setting your price. Perhaps you think that, because Spanish property is selling very briskly in 2000, you can get a very high price. Your agent will know what the market is in your area. You can then decide if you want to put a higher price and wait longer to sell, or a lower price in order to attract an immediate buyer. Be warned that an agent will not work very hard to market your property if he thinks it is overpriced and unlikely to sell.

A good estate agent will see you through the entire process of finding a buyer, negotiating the price, making the contract, securing the payment, signing before the notary, paying the necessary taxes, and all the other details that arise. One frequent pattern is for the seller and buyer to agree all the details of the purchase on what is called a "private contract", at which time the buyer makes a substantial deposit. This deposit takes your property off the market and holds it while the buyer assembles the full amount of the purchase price, either from his own resources or by obtaining a mortgage. If the buyer does not complete the sale, he loses his deposit. If you, the seller, accept a higher offer in the meantime, you have to return double the amount of the deposit.

Be warned. It is astonishing how often an apparently serious purchaser is unable to come up with the cash. Don't count your chickens before they have hatched. Be warned also that many buyers will try to make stage payments and get possession. If they do not complete the payments, you will have plenty of trouble getting them out and recovering your property. (See section below on Lawyers).

When the two parties are ready to complete the sale, they go to the Spanish *Notario* and sign the sales contract at his office.

The contract can also be signed by proxy. This often happens with an absentee seller. He gives his lawyer a power of attorney, called a *poder* in Spanish. This *poder* empowers the attorney to sign in the name of his client. A seller who does not wish to return to Spain can even make this proxy at the Spanish consulate in his own country. People sometimes make a general power of attorney, allowing the holder to dispose of assets as he wishes. This, of course, is not a good idea. Make sure that your *poder* only authorises the holder to sign a specific contract.

This sales contract is then stamped by the *Notario* and it should be immediately taken to the Property Registry office, where it is converted into the famous *escritura* — the title deed. The contract is called an *escritura de compraventa,* a purchase contract, and the title deed is called an *escritura publica,* because it is a registered document of public record. They are exactly the same document, before and after its registration. The original deed is then kept at the notary's office. You yourself never have it. You have only an official copy.

It is only this public deed that makes the buyer the new owner, with a title proof against all comers. Discuss the entire procedure step by step with your agent, so you know what is going on at each stage.

Don't forget that you want a proper bill — *factura* — from your estate agent, listing the amount of the commission and adding 16 per cent IVA to this sum. The entire amount is deductible from your profit as a legitimate expense when you go to calculate your capital gains tax.

## 2. LAWYER

Conventional wisdom says that the buyer always needs a lawyer but the seller may not. We say that the seller, in the complex world of international property transfer, really ought to have a lawyer, too. Your estate agent may be perfectly competent, but complications can arise outside his area of expertise. It is always good to have two people working for you as well so you can compare and contrast their views.

Do you know that some buyers will make you an offer of renting with option to buy with the sole intention of getting a cheap rental? They pay you a low rent, and then they stop paying the rent altogether, and then they leave. They had no intention ever of buying the place. And it isn't worth the expense for you to try to collect the last three or four months of rent that they didn't pay, even if you could find them. Furthermore, your property has been off the market for six months or a year.

So, when the term of option to buy is mentioned, you or your lawyer or your estate agent should be aware that it ought to mean that the buyer pays you two or three million pesetas for this option, which will be deducted from the total price when they purchase. If they let the time limit of the option expire, which might be two or three months, they forfeit what they have paid for it.

Your lawyer will also help you to make a carefully-drawn contract. How will you divide the fees and taxes? Sales contracts often state that the purchaser will pay all taxes and fees. Did you know that Spanish law says that the seller should pay the *plus valía* tax and the Notary and the buyer should pay the transfer tax and the Property Registry fee?

Your lawyer will also explain to you some things not expressed specifically in this contract. Some property transfers are quite clear-cut and no problems arise. Others turn into nightmares.

Lawyer's fees vary widely. You can take one per cent of the purchase price as a guideline for a standard property transfer. Get this clear with your lawyer before you even start. Ask him how much he will charge you. Your legal fees are also deductible from your profits as a necessary expense in realizing your capital gain.

## 2. CONTRACT

For example, your contract may state that your buyer pays ten million pesetas now and takes possession of the property, paying another five million after three months and another five million after an additional three months to complete a total price of 20 million pesetas. If he fails to meet any payment, he forfeits the amount already paid and the property returns to you. He promises to vacate immediately. You don't like the idea of the stage payments, but you feel safe because of this clause in your contract.

Well, your lawyer will warn you that this clause is not strictly enforceable and matters will not turn out so easily if the buyer fails to complete payment. If the buyer can't pay and refuses to leave, you will have to go to court to resolve your contract and get your property back. It will not happen automatically.

The court will probably rule that you indeed get your property back, but that you can't keep all of the 10 or 15 million pesetas the buyer has already paid you. After the court makes its own calculation of how long the buyer has been in the house, plus inconvenience to you, and a series of other factors, it will decide that you can keep, say, five million pesetas only. Then, after this procedure has dragged out for months, you can again take possession of the property and start again on the process of selling it. This is only one of the many, many complications that come up in property transactions.

Some other points you want to study beforehand will be the division of payment of the transfer taxes and fees. Will you follow Spanish regulations and charge the notary and the *plus valía* tax to the seller and the transfer tax and the registration fee to the buyer? Or will you try to make the buyer responsible for all charges in the transfer? What price will you declare, the real price or a lower figure? (See below for more details on these questions).

A good contract will help you foresee and avoid some of these complications but even the best contract cannot protect you against every eventuality. The standard contract used by your estate agent is probably as good as any, but your lawyer may have suggestions to make in your own particular case.

## 4. DECIDE HOW MUCH TO DECLARE

It was formerly a common practice in Spain to declare a property sale at much lower than its real price, in order to save money on transfer tax and wealth tax later. Since the enactment of the law on public fees, which makes an undervaluation of 20 per cent punishable by surcharges, and since the tax ministry's stricter application of all the rules, this practice has largely ceased. If Hacienda believes that your sale is undervalued — and they have their own tables of market values — they may send you a notice that your sale has been reassessed by them, along with a bill for how much extra tax you owe. Today, most contracts are declared at their real value. Furthermore, as buyers become more sophisticated, they have realized that a low declaration now means that they will show a larger profit on paper when they go to sell later, making them subject to a higher Spanish capital gains tax.

If you want to know exactly how much Hacienda thinks your property is worth, you can find out by asking at your regional *oficina liquidadora*. They will give you the amount listed in their own tables. Any attempt to declare a value under that figure will probably bring you a notice to pay more.

Furthermore, if Hacienda reckons that the under declaration exceeds 20 per cent of their calculated value of the property, they can bill you, the seller, for an unjustified capital gain, which draws tax at 35 per cent for the non-resident.

That is, if you declare the sale at 15 million pesetas, but Hacienda calculates the market value of the property at 20 million pesetas, they will charge the seller 35 per cent of five million pesetas, or about 1.7 million pesetas. In addition, they can assume the buyer has received a gift worth five million pesetas and assess gift tax on him of about one million pesetas.

## 5. ASSEMBLE YOUR DOCUMENTS

It will help your sale to go smoothly if you have all your documents in order before you even begin to advertise. It builds confidence in the possible buyer — and his own lawyer — to see all the right papers in order when they consider purchasing. So, what will you need?

### *ESCRITURA PUBLICA*

The most basic paper of all is your title deed, which shows that you are the registered owner of record with an incontestable title. In fact, you have probably never seen your real title deed. What you have is an authorized copy. Unlike some systems of property registration, in Spain it is not the piece of paper itself which counts; it is the inscription in the *Registro de la Propiedad,* the property registry office. If you lose your deed, you can always get another copy from the Notary, where it is on file permanently. Listed on the inscription in the property registry are any liens, charges or mortgages against the property. Back taxes, however, are not listed. Your prospective purchaser will get for himself a *nota simple* from the registry, which is an extract showing the basic information and any charges against the property, but he will want to look at your copy of the full deed in any case.

In a few cases, owners have their property only on a private contract and the house may not even be registered. If this includes you, don't panic. This can be solved in various ways, depending on the individual circumstances. You can offer your buyer the possibility of a Regulation 205 procedure or a full-scale *expediente de dominio, (see reference in this chapter)* in which a court will study the case, publish the proceedings, and finally issue a clear title to the property. You might even find a new buyer willing to run the same risks as you in order to avoid taxes, who will simply purchase the property on a new private contract.

## *IBI RECEIPT*

Your receipt for the paid-up *Impuesto sobre Bienes Inmuebles,* the Real Estate Tax, is an important item. The IBI receipt shows first that the estate tax is paid for this year. It would be a good idea to have the receipts for the last five years, to show good faith. The IBI receipt also shows the amount of the *valor catastral,* the official assessed value of the property for tax purposes. This value is almost always less than the real market value, but they are gradually being raised. The IBI receipt also confirms that the house exists and is registered for taxes, which can be an important point when no *escritura publica* exists and the owner holds the property only by virtue of a private contract. Finally, the IBI must be presented when you sign the contract at the Notary because it also displays the number of the *referencia catastral,* which, since 1997, is a required part of the documentation in property transfers.

## *REFERENCIA CATASTRAL*

The Catastral Reference is the file number of the property's registration in the land registry, which in Spanish is called the catastro, a word that exists but is rarely used in English, and which means the land registry. Property is registered here by its measurements and boundaries and physical characteristics. The Property Registry is concerned with ownership and mortgages. You are right if you think that it doesn't make sense to have two separate bodies — which don't even talk to each other — dealing with land and property registration. Now, even the Spanish authorities begin to agree with you and, as a first step, they require that the catastral reference number accompany any property transfer. Furthermore, the Notary and the Property Registry office are now authorized to make note of the fact if there is any great difference in the physical description of the property given in the catastro and the legal description given in the sales contract and title deed. This difference might include the fact that the catastro shows a four-bedroom villa and a swimming pool while the sales contract mentions only a plot of land at a very low price.

It is yet to be seen just how effectively the Notary and the Registrar of Property will inform the tax office, but the way is now clear, so be warned.

It is a good idea for the seller to obtain the completely detailed certificate of the *referencia catastral* and include it in his documentation. This will add to the prospective purchaser's confidence, and will make it absolutely clear what he is buying.

Land descriptions on the title deeds are often quite vague, even misleading. The catastro is usually more accurate, because they have been updating their information for some years now, sending inspectors to check the physical reality of land and houses, and using aerial photographs as well.

## *INCOME TAX DECLARATION*

As part of your residence status, you will now be required to present your most recent income tax declaration. This will show that you have paid your property owner's imputed income tax, based on an imaginary income of 2 per cent of the assessed value of your property, and your Spanish wealth tax, if the property has a real market value of more than 18 million pesetas, or 36 million pesetas if it is owned in two names, as for a married couple.

If you are a non-resident, you present your current Form 214, on which you declare each year for the same property owner's income tax as well as the wealth tax, which you must pay because you do not have the exemption of 18 million pesetas per individual. The tax declaration is actually more important than the residence permit in showing that you are a tax resident.

## NON-RESIDENCE CERTIFICATE

This belongs to the buyer, not to the seller, but be warned that, if the buyer is a non-resident and the form of payment is not through a bank cheque which identifies the buyer as the issuer, along with his bank, the buyer must obtain beforehand a certificate of non-residence from the Spanish Ministry of the Interior, and it can take as long as two months for this certificate to be issued. That is, if payment takes place abroad, for example, by transfer from the buyer's account in London to your own account in London, this is perfectly legal, but it offers the Spanish tax man no control over the transaction for documentation purposes. So, they require this certificate.

If the buyer works through a Spanish bank, he will have a certificate of changing the foreign money into pesetas for property purchase, and Spain can document the transaction. If the sale takes place in pounds outside Spain, this is perfectly legal, and acceptable as long as the cheque is presented when the deal is completed at the Spanish Notary. It is only when the buyer himself wishes to keep the details anonymous and confidential that he must present the certificate of non-residence.

Spain wants to know where the money comes from, or at least that someone has made a deal without telling them.

## TAXES AND FEES

We have mentioned before the two taxes and two fees on property sales. The two taxes are the ITP — the transfer tax of 6 per cent — and the *plus valía,* a sort of artificial capital gains tax charged on the increase in an official set of values for the property. (See earlier discussion of transfer costs in this chapter) When you are setting your sales price, you will want to take these amounts into consideration.

Remember the Notary and the Property Registry will cost about 50,000 pesetas each for a sale valued at 10 million pesetas. The rates, from the official tables, go up after that. You can find out exactly how much by asking. The *plus valía* varies widely, depending on the amount of time that has passed between sales, as we mentioned earlier. You can find out exactly how much it will be by asking at your Town Hall. They have a *plus valía* office which will tell you the exact amount of the tax beforehand. Once you know these figures, you can compute how much cash you will have left after your sales expenses are deducted. For residents, remember 75 per cent of the *plus valía* is deductible from your income tax.

## COMMUNITY CHARGES AND STATUTES

If you are selling a flat or townhouse that belongs to a Community of Property Owners, you will want to include your last bill for the *cuota* — the community yearly charge, along with a copy of the Statutes that regulate your community. The buyer will want to know what the yearly charge is and he will want to see the Statutes of the community he is joining. It would be a good idea to have a copy of the minutes of the last Annual General Meeting as well, to prove to your prospective purchaser that your community is well-run and a nice place to live.

## SERVICE BILLS

Copies of your bills for rubbish, water, electricity and even telephone are necessary parts of your sales presentation. Any buyer will want to know how much these charges are on the property, and he will also want to be sure that they are paid up.

Once you have assembled all this paperwork, if you are still in the mood to sell your Spanish property, it would be a good idea to prepare a folder with photocopies of each relevant document, so that your or your lawyer or your estate agent will be prepared to answer any question that a prospective buyer might have.

# CONTENTS

# CONTENTS

# Building Your House

If you intend to build your own castle in Spain, the first item on your list should be finding a good lawyer.

This may sound backwards, but when you check out the list below of all the things that can go wrong with buying property, getting a building permit, and contracting the construction, perhaps you will agree.

The second item on your list should be a promise to yourself that you are prepared to put a lot of your own time into overseeing the entire project, from beginning to end. Getting what you want depends on your own personal supervision.

Most building projects in fact go up just as planned, with only minor setbacks, but it is best to be prepared and take care before you start.

So, let's suppose that you are determined to buy land and build your dream house. More foreigners than ever are doing this in the year 2000 because of the shortage of quality ready-made villas, and more builders and architects than ever are ready to help you realize your dream.

The rewards are great. But be prepared for plenty of exasperation and, above all, don't leap in with your eyes shut.

Too often, the aspiring house-builder thinks that all he has to do is pick one model of villa from a selection that the developer or builder shows him, and that it will appear as if by magic a few months later. Well, sometimes this method works out perfectly well.

However, not all of us can read a plan and visualize the final result with accuracy. Too many people tell their builder that House Type B suits them very well, pay a fat deposit, and go back to their native country. When they return six or eight months later, they find that House Type B doesn't look anything like they thought it would; that the builder hasn't placed it in the spot they had agreed on and, furthermore, they absolutely hate the yellow tiles in the bathroom.

It will take your personal supervision to get it done the way you want it. With some forethought and patient attention to detail, you can indeed have your dream house. But let me repeat that first warning. You simply cannot walk away and expect to return finding that your house has been built just the way you want it. You will have to be there every day. Let me repeat. Every day.

First, however, you have to find the land. Everything mentioned in the previous chapter about buying property applies here, and there is more besides. Let's take it step by step.

Let's suppose that you have found a piece of land that suits you. It probably is located in an existing urbanization, or property development. But it may be a corner of Juan's farm two kilometres down a country road. As the Costas and the islands grow ever more developed, ever more people in search of peace and quiet are heading inland, where quiet valleys and hills await them, with lower prices, too.

## Building Permit

The first thing you have to know is, can you get permission from the Town Hall to build on it? There are unexpected zoning changes from time to time, and you may find your beautiful property is in the middle of a green zone where no building can take place, or in a rural area where no new construction is permitted. Or you may find that only on a plot twice as large as what you want will you be allowed to build a house. You or your lawyer can find out from the town hall *urbanismo* department if building permits are being issued.

Do NOT believe the seller. Your Town Hall's *urbanismo* department is a very important stop for you. Go yourself and take someone who speaks Spanish. Your lawyer, for example.

The *permiso de obra* might cost you four per cent of the estimated construction cost, or somewhat more or less, depending on your own municipality.

**PGOU:** You want to see the PGOU, the *Plan General de Ordenación Urbana,* the Town Plan. These in general are approved every four years. Any interim changes in them must be publicly posted and approved, with a chance for affected property owners to protest or make claims.

In many municipalities, especially along the Spanish Costas, you may find that lots of changes have been made in the building codes and Town Plans, sometimes being approved by the Town Hall but still needing the final go-ahead from the regional government, which must vet and clear the municipal plans. In some cases, there are special building codes set up for specific zones. The PGOU analysis is not for amateurs. You need a specialist to make really sure you understand it.

If your land is located in an existing and approved urbanization, the permit will probably be forthcoming, but you must still check on it. You must also be sure that the urbanization is an approved one. There are some developments that never received official approval and where building is stopped today because they never met the legal requirements for the services they must provide, such as roads of a certain width, or water supply. You can find out by asking to see the *proyecto de urbanización* and the *plan parcial,* or the plan of parcels, at the town hall.

Be SURE to check also the building regulations for plots and areas around your chosen spot. One of the worst, and most frequent, horror stories on the fast-growing coasts of Spain is the nightmare of the cutoff view. That is, you return to your pleasant villa on a hillside overlooking the Mediterranean to discover that a four-storey apartment building now blocks your view, and your new neighbours look right into your bedroom window. Make sure that you know what type of building permits will be issued around you before you buy.

In the brisk building climate today, this may be more complicated than it sounds. In some municipalities the urban planning authorities even make special deals with developers, whereby land is rezoned to permit greater building in exchange for part of the builder's profits going into the Town's coffers. This is neither illegal nor corrupt, as the profits help all residents of the town, but it can harm the interests of those who already have purchased.

A wave of protest has arisen in Marbella, for example, where the Town Plan provides for enormous amounts of new building, enough to triple the population in the next eight years. Current residents charge that some present building permits have been granted for land zoned for parks and schools, and that such rapid new building will lower the quality of life in the town.

Be sure to talk with your new neighbours before you sign any contracts.

## Country Land

If your land is in the deep country, you will need to check on other factors at the town hall, such as whether you need to buy, say, 10,000 square metres of land before you can build, or whether any encumbrances exist.

There might be a *camino real* or a *servidumbre de paso,* an old pathway that crosses the land. It is a right of way and you can't cut it by building. People can pass over your land and it might even be transformed into a road some day. Or an irrigation ditch might exist, which again is a legal right of way you cannot block, nor can you deny access to it for those who use it. Country land may have water problems, too. Where does the water come from? Can it be cut off?

Have an expert check the town planning maps to see if any new highways are planned for the zone. It can come as a nasty surprise five years later when you see the bulldozers starting work next door, or you are called to a hearing where expropriation proceedings will start to take the bottom of your garden.

Once you have determined that a building permit will be forthcoming and that no special encumbrances exist on the land, you can start to find out just what land you are buying.

The seller must have an *escritura* for the land, just as for a flat or land with an existing house. As we mentioned in the preceding chapter, sometimes there is no registered title for the land, only a private document. See the preceding chapter for various ways of getting the land officially registered.

But, in the more usual case where official title exists, this *escritura pública* will describe the land, but sometimes the description isn't exact enough to suit you. Descriptions in the Property Registry often use vague terms like the bare statement that the land borders on the east with the land of Pepe Garcia. Well, Pepe Garcia has a big farm. Just what part of it constitutes the border? It could be where the fence is or where the ditch is or where the path is.

So then you will need an official survey. Remember that the Property Registry is concerned with ownership, not with exact description. A surveyor is called a *topografo* and he will measure your plot exactly. You can have this done independently but you should also check the catastral registry.

**Check the Catastro**

Here again, just as with buying a house, you want to check with the *Catastro* as well as the Property Registry. The Catastral Office lists the boundaries and measurements and physical characteristics of the land. You want to be sure that this description squares with the description in the *escritura*. If not, you may be able to get the catastral reference to square with the reality of the land, and this in turn with the title deed.

The *Catastro* will have a map, a plan of the land, so that you can see that the boundary with Pepe Garcia's farm runs along the fence, just as you might think. Or you might see that your plot includes some triangle of what Pepe Garcia thinks belongs to him. Especially in old country properties, there is often some confusion.

You want to have exact, officially recognized boundaries, and the number of square metres the same on the survey and the *escritura*. They probably will not agree, but you can correct this when you purchase, so that your own title and the physical description are in agreement. This clarity will be greatly to your benefit should you later wish to sell your land and house.

Ask for the official surveyor at the town hall. The survey will form part of your *escritura* when you buy the land. If your land is on an approved urbanization, there will likely be an up-to-date survey already existing. The survey and the *plan parcial* will also show your access and where your water and electricity come from.

Once you have determined that you can indeed build and you know the exact borders of your land, you had better find out if the seller is in fact the owner of the land. Are you buying from the developers of the urbanization, or from an individual? If the land is in the *campo,* does Juan really own it? He may share it with his two brothers, one of whom does not want to sell. Or there may be a mortgage on it. The same rules apply as for any property purchase. Check the *Registro de la Propiedad.*

Finally, you sign the *escritura de compraventa* at the *notario,* and you are ready to proceed with building. When you checked restrictions at the town hall, you should also have discovered what building code problems you may have. Do you have to leave three metres between your boundary and any building? Can you put a wall closer to the road than one metre? Is two storeys the absolute limit? If you are in an established urbanization, does the association of property owners require you to submit your building plans for approval?

We repeat that checking the building code sounds simple but in practice it is often complicated. Many municipalities have old building codes in place, with new ones written and approved by the Town Council, but not yet ratified by their Regional Governments, which must give final approval. So *permisos de obra*, or building permits, are sometimes granted on the basis of shaky legality. In addition, it is common to find that some zones have special regulations within the main system. You really want an expert with local knowledge to check on this.

## Building Can Be Simple

In spite of the possible problems we have listed above, the building itself might be very easy. Many of the larger urbanisation will put you in touch with two or three building contractors who work regularly with them. They will show you several models of homes, together with their prices and specifications, all included, from site preparation to curtain selection. You pick out what you want; suggest a few personal needs and changes; agree to payment terms, and then all you need is to check on progress from time to time, and make sure they are giving you what they promised. This is the easy way. It's a little more expensive, because all this service costs money and even then you have to keep checking up to make sure you are getting what was promised.

Perhaps you want a home that you yourself have designed. You sit on the land for a while and you get some ideas. You want a terrace here for the view, and the pool in that fold of land. You want the bedrooms along the back and the living-room in the front, facing south to the sea. None of the ready-made designs suit you.

## Architect Is Necessary

Now you need an architect. You have your rough sketches but you need someone who can turn them into real blueprints. In fact, you will need architect's drawings in order to get your building permit in any case.

The only way to find a good architect is to ask around. If you prefer to use a foreign architect for your design, you may do so. Since Spain's entry into Europe, EU architects can now practise and sign plans for approval by the official *Colegio de Arquitectos*.

Architects' fees, at least as a minimum, are standard and are set by the *Colegio*. They are about 6 per cent of the estimated cost of construction.

To this you must add another 3 per cent for the *aparejador* (see next page), so your design and supervision will cost you about 9 per cent of your estimated construction cost. This construction cost, by the way, will be less than either your real cost or the real market value of the house when finished.

The price includes final plans that must suit you, and the six copies necessary for approval by the College of Architects and for your building permit. The six and three per cent figures are no longer obligatory, but are only suggested minimum charges, as the College no longer has the legal power to enforce the rates. Hence, you may be able to get a cheaper fee by a little negotiating.

## *Memoria* **Is a Binding Agreement**
## *for Building Specifications*

The price also includes preparation of the *memoria,* or building specifications, which includes items like the size of pipes, the formula for the concrete, and the type of materials to be used. You yourself want to have a personal hand in this, and you can choose here just what sort of electrical fittings and bathroom fixtures and kitchen tiles you want. This is the time to think of details about shelves and about whether you want wood window frames or aluminium, and so on.

It is important to give this a great deal of thought because the *memoria* is what you will give your builder in order to get his bid on the job. He will set his price according to the materials stated in the *memoria,* and any changes you may make later, or any additions, will cost you extra. These extras can add up to a lot of money, so the *memoria* is a very important document.

The architect's fee includes overall supervision of the construction, but you are not likely to see your architect on the building site once he has finished the design. The actual supervision falls to the *aparejador,* a professional architectural engineer who sees that the building is carried out to the specifications required. He will visit the site from time to time to check on things and he will take his own fee, about half what the architect charges you. He signs the documents certifying that the house is properly constructed, which you will need in order to occupy your house legally and to get your electricity connected.

Your architect will be able to recommend an *aparejador*. Often they work out of the same office.

Finally, you are ready to find a builder. It is only reasonable to get several bids on your job, remembering that the lowest bid is not always the best deal and that the highest bid does not ensure high quality. Ask around.

Your contract with the builder should include the *memoria*. It should state the total price; whether or not the site grading and preparation and final clean-up are included; the manner of payment, and give a definite completion date, with a penalty clause for late delivery. You ought to have your lawyer take a look at this contract.

## Payment Schedules Vary

Payment terms are not standard, but a typical schedule might be:

1. A deposit of 20 per cent when the contract is signed.
2. Another 20 per cent when the walls and roof are completed. (At this point, it is customary to have the *bandera* party, when a flag is placed on the roof, and the owner invites the workers and his own friends to a fiesta at the site.)
3. Another 20 per cent when the door and window frames are installed and the inside is more or less complete.
4. Another 20 per cent when the house is painted and ready to inhabit, with plumbing and electricity installed and functioning.
5. A payment of 10 per cent when all the outside work included in the contract is finished, such as patios, walls, pool.
6. The final payment of 10 per cent should be held back for six months to a year, if you can swing the deal, to cover any defects in construction which don't show up until the rains start, for example. There is always something.

Keep in mind that the builder has legal responsibility for hidden defects in the construction for a period of 10 years after completion. Architects and constructors have been sent to jail in Spain when their buildings collapsed before this period.

Now you have your dream house, but there are still two things you must do. One is to register the house for real estate taxes, the *Impuesto sobre Bienes Inmuebles* (IBI).

### Declaración de Obra Nueva

However, in order to do this, you must first make a *declaración de la obra nueva,* a declaration of new work, in order to have the structure appear on your *escritura.* So far, your deed mentions only the piece of land, not the house you have just built.

The declaration of new work will cost you one half of one per cent of the declared value of the construction. Again, if Hacienda does not agree with your declared value, they can raise it.

Your lawyer or property consultant will show you how to register the new house. If you do not register *(dar de alta)* with the tax people, you can be fined, so take care of it as soon as possible. Two per cent of the value of your house is also calculated as income when you go to file for your Spanish income tax.

When you go to make your declaration of new work and register the house, you will need the *certificado final de obra* issued by the architect, the *licencia de obra ,* building permit, issued by the town hall, and the *licencia de primera ocupación,* the permit to inhabit the dwelling, from the town hall.

A non-resident builder must also present a bank certificate showing that he has imported the funds from abroad and changed them into pesetas. The purpose of the certificate is to make sure that the non-resident is not using black money earned inside Spain for his building.

Then you will be the completely legal owner of your dream house and you can begin to pay both property owner's income tax and Spanish wealth tax on your new property.

That is, if you are a non-resident. Since 1999, the resident is exempt from property owner's imputed income tax on his principal dwelling, as well as having the exemption of 18 million pesetas on his wealth tax.

CHAPTER FOUR

# CONTENTS

# Rentals in Spain

Spanish lawyers' offices are filled with landlords whose tenants refuse to pay the rent or vacate the flat, and with tenants who cannot get the landlords to repair the leaky roof.

Many, many problems arise with rentals. If you hope to let your Spanish property and make some money to help pay your mortgage, you will have to take a few precautions because Spanish law in general favours the tenant.

Yet even tenants can find that they wind up paying high rents for properties that have not been properly maintained and that Spanish courts take a long time to compel the landlords to make repairs.

Let's take a look at each situation, but first we need a little background.

### *Ley de Arrendamientos Urbanos*

Spain's current Law of Urban Lettings, the *Ley de Arrendamientos Urbanos,* went into effect on January 1, 1995, but many renters and letters, especially foreigners, are still unaware of its provisions.

The law brought some good news for those Spanish property owners who are still stuck with sitting tenants under the pre-1985 law, and it also brought good news for tenants who were victims of arbitrary rent rises under the law in force from 1985 to 1995.

The 1995 law ends a maze of contradictory Spanish legislation which made life difficult for tenants and landlords alike and all but ruined the rental property market in Spain.

Two of its main provisions will make life easier for both landlords and tenants.

1.  The current law ends the forcible extension provision of the 1964 law, which made rental contracts indefinitely renewable by the tenant. The new law allows landlords gradually to raise the old controlled and ri-

diculously low rents of the 1964 law to market prices today, and, eventually, to recover their own property.

2. The law also provides tenants with more security than the 1985 law stipulated, now obliging landlords to renew residential rental contracts for up to five years.

## Three Rental Situations

We find that we have to distinguish three possible situations for rentals in Spain today, depending on when the contract was made.

## 1964-1985

Under the terms of the rental laws in effect from 1964 to 1985 tenants were so protected that landlords gave up in despair and stopped building rental apartments, which led to a critical housing shortage. More than half a million apartments in Spain are still occupied under this old law, which protected a tenant so strongly that he could pass on his rights to his children and even his grandchildren. Further, his rent could never be raised, or raised only by a small percentage related to the inflation rate.

Would you believe there are more than 500,000 apartments in Spain whose tenants pay less than 5,000 pesetas a month? There are buildings in Madrid where the grandchildren of the original tenants are living in spacious flats in prestigious areas, paying rents of 1,000 pesetas a month while, until 1985, the landlord was helpless to do anything about it, even though his real estate tax is 250,000 pesetas a year and his community fees are another l00,000. Next door, another tenant may be paying 200,000 pesetas a month for the same type of apartment, having signed his contract after 1985.

Some foreign property owners on the Spanish Mediterranean coasts fell into this trap before 1985. Thinking to make a little money on their holiday flat or eventual retirement home, they rented it out, with a contract for some specific time period.

Later they were horrified to discover that their tenants refused to vacate and had become entitled to the forcible extension of their contracts, regardless of the landlord's desire to end the letting and recover his property.

Many landlords chose to leave their apartments empty rather than risk the dangers of a sitting tenant. Landlords refused to repair the crumbling buildings which brought them no profit, and nobody would even think of constructing new rental property.

## 1985

Revised rental laws passed in 1985 by the Socialist government aimed to remedy this situation in the best capitalist way, by making rental properties good business. The revised law provided that all contracts ended when they said they ended, without provision for forcible extension. The law also ended any restrictions on rent increases. Landlords immediately began to raise rents sharply and to offer short-term contracts with little protection for the tenant. Now it was the tenants who suffered, because they were unwilling to settle into a flat from which they might be evicted in one year's time, or be forced to pay sharp increases.

## 1995

The 1995 rental law now in force is designed to provide a better balance between the rights and needs of tenants and landlords and to bring at last a final solution to the generations of sitting tenants.

If you are one of the foreign property owners stuck with a sitting tenant, you are now able to recover your property. Don't cheer too loudly, however, because it can take you the tenant's lifetime, plus two years. However, you will be able to raise the rent to a normal level over either five years or 10 years, depending on the tenant's income.

If the tenant earns less than 4.6 million pesetas a year, his rent can be gradually raised to market levels over 10 years. If he earns more than that, his rent can be raised in five years to a market figure.

The old-law tenant still has the right to pass on the apartment to his spouse or children. And they can pass it on to their children, but only for two years. After that, the landlord will at last be able to take possession of his own property. In the meantime, of course, he will have been able to raise the rent to the price levels of today.

Landlords in this position should take legal advice from property specialists in order to make sure they are effectively exercising their rights.

There are a number of legal steps that each landlord must take before he can begin raising his rents, such as citing the tenant to declare his income. If the tenant does not respond, the landlord can then begin raising the rent to bring it to a market level within five years, the faster option.

## Five-year Contract

On the side of tenant protection today, the present law provides that residential contracts, as distinct from short-term holiday lets, must have a minimum duration of five years.

That is, a landlord can offer a contract of two years or three years, but, if the tenant decides that he wants to stay on, this contract is renewable annually for a total period of five years. If the tenant himself wishes a contract of only two or three years, this is all right.

The rent can be revised upward by an inflation factor each year. At the end of the five years, the landlord can raise the rent as much as he chooses, either for his new tenant or for his existing tenant, if he decides to stay on at the new and higher rent.

## Deposit

The new letting law also establishes, for the first time in law, the landlord's right to a deposit as a guarantee against damages. The deposit can be held by an agency independent of both landlord and tenant. This agency will not release the deposit until both parties agree.

The deposit consists of one month's rent for an unfurnished apartment, two months' rent for a furnished apartment, and two months' rent for commercial premises.

The deposit, called a *fianza,* can be held by the housing department of the regional government. In Andalusia, for example, it is deposited with the *Consejería de la Vivienda* of the Andalusian autonomous government, which has offices in major cities.

## Registered Contract

For full security in your rental, you also want your rental contract registered with the same body. This means that you will have full legal protection in the event of any court case about your rental. Let's face it; most rental contracts, especially with foreigners, are simply not registered and the landlords are probably not declaring the rental income for tax purposes. Your contract is still valid in court, but only the registered contract, where the landlord is completely legal in his operations, has the full protection of the law.

It is never a good idea to pay the deposit directly into the landlord's account, as he then is in complete control over whether to release the deposit or not at the end of the let, but it is a common practice.

## Holiday Rentals
### *Have Separate Rules*

The new law does not affect short-term holiday rental contracts, called *arrienda de temporada.* These holiday contracts do not grant the tenant any right to automatic extension and they require that the tenant vacate when the contract ends.

So, foreign property owners can be assured of this legal protection when they let their holiday homes for periods of several months. However, they should still take some care with vetting tenants because the legal procedures for eviction of a tenant who refuses to leave can take more than six months, even when the law is on the landlord's side.

There have been a number of recent cases in which unscrupulous tenants have signed up for holiday rentals, say, for two months, and then simply remained in the apartment without paying any further rent. Four to six months later, the landlord is able to obtain an eviction order, but the tenants have lived rent-free for that period. Even though a court enters a judgment against them for the amount of rent owed, they simply move to another town and repeat the scheme.

If you decide to rent in Spain, you will find thousands of apartments and villas at prices to suit every pocket.

Some of them are very basically-equipped little flats designed for self-catering holidays and often rented through agents in Britain, Holland or Germany. Others are real homes, being let by their owners in the hope of making a little money from their property until they can retire to enjoy it full time.

For those coming to Spain to live, it is a good idea to rent a place in the area where they hope to live permanently, so they can make a careful survey of local conditions before buying. Renting may also be the best plan for people whose capital is in sound investments and who do not wish to tie it up in property.

When you have found a flat or a villa which suits your needs, you will be asked to sign a rental contract.

## Foreign Contract

If you are renting a holiday flat for a self-catering visit to Spain, you will probably find this contract in your own language, to be signed in your own country before you leave with the rental company handling the property.

This is perfectly all right. Just make sure the rental company has a sound reputation. Sometimes the accommodation promised you does not measure up to your expectations, so be alert. See below for How to Complain in Spain.

The contract forms are usually quite standard, including a list of all the equipment and furnishings, and requiring a deposit to cover any damages the tenant may cause. There is not normally any dispute about the return of this deposit if you have left the flat in good condition.

If you have seen the way some holidaymakers leave their rented flats, you would understand why the companies insist on this deposit.

## Spanish Contract

If you are already in Spain when you rent, you will also be asked to sign a contract. It will specify the amount of the rent, the manner of payment, any deposit and the time period.

The contract will be headed, *por temporada,* which means short-term. This is to distinguish it from a long-term rental, called *vivienda,* or residence, because long-term tenants have rights which short-term tenants do not.

### *Temporada, Vivienda* Tenants
### *Have Different Rights*

A *temporada* contract might even be as long as one year. There is no specific time limit past which a contract becomes long-term.

However, unless otherwise specified in your short-term rental contract, the landlord may put you out at the end of the period stated, or he may offer you a new contract increasing the rent as much as he likes.

These short-term contracts are designed for holiday rentals, not as long-term or permanent residence. Such a *temporada* contract running for one year would be pushing it a little, but the idea is to show the intention of impermanence, so the tenant does not establish full rights. This does not always work as planned, as in the example that follows. Short-term tenants can sometimes claim a longer contract.

The *vivienda* contract, on the other hand, is meant for those long-term lets when the tenant truly makes the apartment his home. The tenant is much more protected and Spanish law requires that a *vivienda* contract be granted for a minimum period of five years.

This gives the tenant some stability, as he knows that he has at least this period, and he must be officially notified well in advance of the end of the period if the landlord does not intend to renew the contract.

During the period of 1985-1995, the rental laws stated that landlords were free to offer any sort of contract they desired, for any length of time they liked. There was, and still is, a shortage of good rental apartments in Spain, so the landlords took advantage of the situation and offered short contracts, often of one year only, with stiff rent increases at each renewal.

The current law, with its five-year minimum, has corrected this imbalance.

There are disadvantages for the long-term tenant also. Longer-term, or *vivienda*, contracts often contain provisions requiring the tenant to pay community fees, that is, the dues charged each year by the property owners' collective for that block of flats, and even the real estate taxes, known as the IBI.

An owner is within his rights to make such a contract, but you should be wary and know what you are getting into. Such extra charges can add up. Furthermore, clauses obliging the tenant to pay the community fees and real estate taxes are considered abusive under Spanish law, and you can protest if you choose, even after you have signed the contract.

If these charges are not mentioned in your contract, they are the owner's responsibility and you can refuse any attempt by him to make you pay for them.

To sum up, in strictly legal terms, the taxes and fees are for the property owner's account. However, it is not illegal for the landlord and tenant to agree in the contract that the tenant will pay them. As long as you know what you are getting into, and the amounts of these charges are clear, and you as the tenant are disposed to accept the price, then it is okay.

If, however, you feel that you have been deceived by the landlord into signing the contract, you can protest the clause and you will surely win your case.

So, we see that the current rental laws aim to provide fair treatment for both landlords and tenants, with safeguards for each party to the contract.

However, as soon as a new law is made, someone will try to find a way around it for their own benefit.

## Traps for Both Tenant and Landlord

For example, landlords who don't want to tie up their property for the legal five-year minimum have taken to offering their tenants a short-term contract under the *temporada* heading, even when the tenant wants a long-term *vivienda* contract. Some tenants have signed these contracts because rental flats are in short supply and they needed a place to live. Here the landlord is taking advantage of the tenant, denying him the right to a five-year contract, and leaving the way open for rent increases at the end of the year.

Some tenants simply accept this practice, but others get legal advice and go to court. The tenant declares that he signed this one-year contract under the short-term *temporada* heading only because he could find no other suitable accommodation, that he lives and works in this city and it is his home, and he asks the court to order his contract extended to the full five years, with only inflationary increases programmed into the rental.

In dozens of cases, the court has ruled in favour of the tenant, forcing the landlord to extend the contract to the five-year minimum.

It doesn't always work this way, however. In several other cases, involving tenants who had not such established roots in a town, the courts have ruled in favour of the landlord and the existing short-term contract.

Each of these cases needs careful study by the court, to determine in fairness whether the tenant or the landlord is trying to take advantage of the other.

## No Contract

You may find a charming little flat by the sea, whose owner doesn't want to make any contracts. This can be perfectly all right, too. Just make sure you have clearly written receipts for the rent you pay, which will constitute an implicit contract.

Such an implicit rental contract exists even if you don't have the receipts, as soon as the owner cashes your cheque, but it's better to have some piece of paper.

If you are paying month to month in such a situation, the implicit contract ends at the end of each month you pay, or on the date stated on your receipt.

### One-Year Contract

#### *Can Favour Tenant*

Let's suppose you want to rent a villa in Spain for a year, or even more, and you find that a rental agency in your home country, or even in Spain, has the perfect house at the right price. They offer you a one-year contract, in German or English, with option to renew. This contract, in your own language, will not say that it is either a *temporada* or a *vivienda* contract. The agency does not think in terms of Spanish law, and they don't expect that you will, either.

This foreign-language contract is perfectly legal, although it would have to be translated into Spanish for any court proceedings, and it is a perfectly good offer, which, in fact gives you as the tenant more protection than it gives the landlord.

If you want to renew your contract, you can, and if the landlord wants you to leave, you can threaten to go to court, claiming that the villa has become your retirement home. You can say that you will ask the court to have the contract extended to the full five years of the long-term let. The landlord and the agency will be reluctant to become involved in any legal dispute in Spanish courts first, because they will probably lose their case, and, secondly, because we can almost certainly assume that they are not declaring all the rental income for Spanish taxes. Even if you pay in marks or pounds in another country, the income derived from property in Spain is still subject to Spanish tax.

### Notification Necessary

Be advised that, if you have a five-year *vivienda* contract and your landlord wishes to terminate your rental at the end of the period, he is obliged to notify you officially, for example, by a notarized letter, well before the end of the period. If he does not notify you officially, the contract can be regarded as renewed for two years and for the same rent.

In any of these situations, most Europeans will find the tenant to have more protection than is normal in many countries. That is, even though the law states that the rental period is finished, a landlord will have some trouble putting out anyone who chooses to stay. He cannot simply summon a policeman and order you out. He must get a court order for this and the procedure will take some time, even when the law is entirely on the landlord's side.

## Rental Complaints

Finally, if you feel that your holiday apartment does not meet the terms of your contract, or if your landlord has abused his side of the deal, you can complain. If you are a genuine tourist, the tourist office of the province or town where the property is located will hear your complaint. If you are a semi-permanent resident, you will do better at the O.M.I.C., the *Oficina Municipal de Información al Consumidor*. This is the consumer information office, usually directed by the regional government. Its mission is to deal with consumer problems and these include rents.

## Landlords Must Be Wary

Landlords, as you can see by the information above, if you wish to let your own flat or villa in Spain, or go into the tourist accommodation business, you must be very careful about the terms of your contracts and the quality of your tenants.

The opportunity to pay off your property by letting it looks tempting on paper. It can work out to your entire satisfaction, and in fact it usually does.

Nevertheless, many problems arise and you need to be wary. Tenants may damage your furniture or harm your plumbing and electrical installations. Letting agents may keep your money and allow your apartment to fall into ruin while you are absent.

Or you might fall into the short-term contract trap described above. In good faith you might rent to a young Spanish man who says he has a six-month work contract in your town, and needs a short-term let. Then he moves in his wife and children, who were not mentioned when he signed the contract, and then he brings his own furniture, and then he goes to court to accuse you of abusing the short-term contract. As he lives and works in the town, the court will probably rule in his favour, and you will have to wait five years to recover your property.

The safest way is to let only to people you know and trust. Even then it is a good idea to get the rent in advance and a deposit against possible damages as well. Electric bills always arrive late, so it is best to include an estimated charge in the rent. If you have a telephone, you will find that having it disconnected and reconnected is an irritating exercise. But it's worth it. You can get a lock for it, but that is never quite sufficient. Perhaps the best idea is to have the sort of phone which you can unplug from the wall and remove. There have been many, many problems with telephones.

## Spanish Tax Due
### on Spanish Rentals

It is quite legal and proper for you, as either a resident or non-resident property owner in Spain, to rent out your property. You must keep in mind, however, that you must declare your rental income for Spanish income tax.

Even if your tenant pays you in Danish kroner before he leaves for Spain, legally this income arises in Spain because the property is in Spain. It is almost certainly true that most owners who let their property occasionally say nothing about it to the tax authorities and the chances of their getting caught are slim. Nevertheless, Spanish income tax is due on any profits arising in Spain.

If you are a non-resident, you are liable for Spanish non-resident income tax of 25 per cent from the very first peseta of rental income, declared on form 210.

If you are a resident, you should add your rental income to your other income when you make your annual Spanish income tax declaration.

But let's suppose that you are interested in more than a few short lets each year on a casual basis. You may find that your garden apartment development or your urbanization office includes a letting service which, for a commission, will handle all the details for you. This could be your solution, but read the agreement carefully and talk to others who have used this service to make sure they are satisfied.

There are also holiday companies which bring people to Spain for two or three week self-catering vacations. These are becoming more and more popular, especially for young families who prefer to stay away from hotels. These companies are always looking for new properties to let. Because they charge their clients high prices for short stays, they can afford to pay you, the owner, a high price for your property.

Again, be sure to read their agreement very carefully. Remember that a series of holiday tenants can do a lot of damage to your property.

Also make sure that this company is legally registered and that it is paying all the proper taxes. Because, when you provide linens and other hotel-type services, and deal with many tourist visitors on a short-term basis, you move into a new area legally. You are now a business yourself and in many tourist areas of Spain, you should legally declare your property as a tourist letting accommodation. This means that inspectors will come to check the standards and the tax man will be informed.

This means that you or your holiday rental company must declare the income, and set aside 25 per cent of the rent as a withholding tax to the Spanish government. You declare this tax on Hacienda form 210. You or your holiday company must also add an extra 16 per cent IVA, value added tax, to the rent, which must be paid to the Finance ministry as well.

On the other hand, you can now deduct maintenance expenses from your Spanish income tax. You cannot do this when you inhabit the property yourself, but maintenance becomes a business expense when you let out your property regularly.

You may also employ a real estate agency in Spain to handle your letting, but be sure you are dealing with people who are competent and whom you trust. All too often one finds that extra fees and charges from the agency soon add up, or they do not properly see to the maintenance of the place.

There have been cases where the agency has rented out the property and told the owner that it was not rented. The agency kept all of the money and the absentee owner assumed that his flat was empty.

Formerly, you could even get stuck with a sitting tenant under the previous regulations. This could happen when a tenant, after a short stay, wanted to renew his contract, or stay a few more months. The owner, or his agent, agreed, and took the tenant's cheque.

Then the owner wanted to come to Spain and enjoy his home for a few months. The tenant refused to vacate. During that time, he had become an official resident of Spain and declared that the house was his new home and he had nowhere else to go. The courts upheld him, under the pre-May 9, 1985 terms, and the landlord was stuck. Many owners are still in this unhappy situation today, although they can at least update the rent over five or 10 years.

## Eviction Is Difficult

Under what conditions can the owner regain his property and put a tenant out?

Some causes are failure to pay the rent (although courts have often ruled that these arrears must exceed six months before any action will be taken), damage to the property, use of the property for immoral purposes, subletting unless agreed in the contract, and the causing of a serious nuisance to the neighbours.

In any case, a court order must be obtained against the tenant and many months will pass before you get him out.

Take note of the advice given above to tenants. If you have let your property on a five-year *vivienda* contract and you wish to take possession yourself at the end of that time, remember that you must officially notify the tenant well before the end of the contract that you do not intend to renew it. If you do not do this correctly, the contract can be regarded as renewed for two years and at the same rent.

## Business Premises

More and more foreigners are coming to Spain to start their own businesses. You can even find full-page advertisements listing bars. All of these bars appear to be doing a great business, and it is a mystery why their present owners want to sell them.

As one foreign resident of the Costa del Sol remarked, "I have never seen a place where businesses appear, and then disappear, so rapidly."

Indeed, many new foreign residents have seen their dreams dashed when their nice little business in the sun went bust.

Not the least of their problems is often the leasing, purchase or rental of the business premises. This is an area where you really need the best legal advice, apart from your normal good business sense.

## Traspaso

This is the famous Spanish leasehold, in which the business operator and holder of the *traspaso* has the right to resell it on to a third party, although he must first offer it to the property owner. If the property owner chooses not to buy back the leasehold at the price asked, the tenant can then sell it to another person, with the landlord having the right to perhaps 10 per cent of the sale.

There are several versions of the *traspaso,* and you will have to read your contract carefully, as each version has some different conditions about the tenant's right to sell on, and about the percentage due to the landlord.

117

The *traspaso* in fact no longer exists under terms of the current letting laws, although the previously constituted leaseholds continue to be valid.

## Cesión

The term for leasehold is now *cesión*, and there is no exact legal format required. That is, a property owner and a business tenant can agree on any conditions they choose, which often means that the deal is much more like a normal rental contract, although it is usually open-ended, with no final cutoff point as long as the tenant continues to pay the rent.

## Watch Out For

Be particularly alert to the terms of any lease or rental contract you purchase from a presently-operating business. Quite often it will be presented as a leasehold when it is simply a rental agreement which gives the tenant no rights to any of the profit from reselling it.

When you are asked to pay 10 or 20 million pesetas for a "leasehold", you want to be very sure that you are buying something which you will later have the right to sell. If all that is being offered is a rental agreement, then you are paying 10 million pesetas for nothing.

This has happened to more than one business purchaser in Spain, who sees the term *traspaso* on the contract heading and believes he is buying a lease, when the contract, when carefully read, turns out to be just a rental.

Be sure to take legal advice before you get into a Spanish lease.

# CONTENTS

# Taxes on Property

## Buyers, Be Warned...
### *You Will Pay Spanish Capital Gains Tax*
CHANGES IN SPANISH tax regulations mean that anyone who buys property in Spain today will be liable to pay Spanish capital gains tax when he sells his flat or villa in the future.

Residents will pay at a maximum 20 per cent and non-residents at 35 per cent of their profits. A non-resident seller will be subject to having five per cent of the total sales price paid directly to Spain's Tax Agency as a deposit against his capital gains liability.

When real estate agents speak glowingly of the brisk and rising market, they give the impression that you are sure to make money when you sell later. They are probably right, but they often forget to mention the Spanish tax picture.

Until December 31, 1996, both residents and non-residents could deduct 11.11 per cent per year from their profits, after the first two years of ownership, and pay no tax at all after 10 years. This favourable picture has now ended.

## Residents Over 65
### *No Longer Must Pay*
The good news in 2000 comes for residents 65 years of age and over, who are now exempt from Spanish capital gains tax when they sell their principal dwelling. If they sell a holiday home, they still face the tax.

This means that, if you are, say, 68 years old and hold a Spanish residence permit, you can buy a principal residence this year and sell it in three years for a fat profit in today's brisk real estate market, and have no capital gains tax to pay.

We don't know if this measure will lead to a wave of geriatric speculation in property, but the possibility exists.

We can distinguish three possible situations for sellers of Spanish property today. These are:

## 1. Long-term Owners

The fortunate long-term owners who bought their homes before December 31, 1986, meaning they have owned them for 10 years before December 31, 1996. They have no Spanish capital gains tax to pay when they sell now and they are not subject to the five per cent retention.

## 2. Transitional Sellers

Those who bought in the period from 1987 through 1994. They have the right to the 11.11 per cent per year reduction, starting after the first two years of ownership, but only up to 1996. Those who bought in 1995 have no reduction because their initial two-year period of no reduction runs up against the December 31, 1996, cutoff point. They can also apply the inflation correction factor (see below).

## 3. Today's Buyers

Those who purchase today (and really, since 1995) will have no reductions at all. Their only help is the application of a coefficient that corrects for inflation, which at today's low inflation, is very small indeed. Nevertheless, it is a help because it is applied to the entire amount of your original purchase price, rather than to the amount of your profit, so you don't pay much more tax than under the old system.

So you can figure that you will pay tax on any profit you make when you sell your Spanish property. You will also, as a non-resident, be subject to the five per cent deposit made to Hacienda when the property is sold, no matter how long you have owned your home in the sun.

### *For Example:*

If you buy a luxury garden apartment today in the year 2000 for 25 million pesetas and sell it in the year 2004 for 30 million pesetas, five years will have passed, and you will have gained five million pesetas. Let's suppose inflation continues very low and let's say it averages only two per cent per year in the new single-currency Europe. So, two times five years gives 10 per cent. You get to add 2.5 million (10 per cent of 25 million) to your original price, making it the same value in pesetas of 2003. Now you have 27.5 million, which you subtract from 30 million, making your taxable profit 2.5 million.

At 35 per cent for non-residents, this makes your tax about 900,000 pesetas. Your purchaser will have deposited five per cent of the total sale price of 30 million, or 1.5 million pesetas, with Spain's Tax Agency to cover your capital gains liability. You have to claim back the extra 600,000 pesetas, which will take a few months at least.

You will have paid the Spanish tax man 900,000 pesetas on your profit of five million pesetas. Your buyer makes the deposit of 5 per cent directly to Hacienda to make sure you pay up.

There is no escape from this, at least until they change the law again.

If you are an official resident of Spain, you will pay as part of your yearly income tax declaration, at the same rate as your income tax. Thus, if you have a modest income and pay Spanish income tax at a rate of 15 per cent, you will also pay your capital gains tax at 15 per cent. If you have a higher income, subject to taxation at 30 or 40 per cent, don't worry too much, because the resident's capital gains tax is limited to a maximum of 20 per cent. Thus, you could never pay more than 500,000 pesetas on your profit of 2.5 million, a better deal than the non-resident gets. The resident can also apply the *coeficiente de actualización,* the inflation correction factor.

See the end of this section for more details on Spanish capital gains tax.

# Taxes You Pay Every Year

## Property Owners Income Tax

### *Annulled for Main Residence*

All property owners in Spain are liable for three separate taxes every year. These taxes are:

1. Property Owners' Imputed Income Tax
2. Wealth Tax
3. Annual Real Estate Tax

## 1. Property Owners' Imputed Income Tax

The good news for residents is that Spain's property owners' imputed income tax disappeared in 1999 for the owner's principal residence.

A non-resident must continue to pay the yearly tax, however, because he is not resident in Spain, so his principal dwelling cannot be here. Residents who own more than one dwelling will also continue to be subject to the tax on their second home or other property.

Persons subject to this tax have two per cent of the *valor catastral*, the official rated value, of their property attributed to them as a sort of imaginary income. This is 1.1 per cent if your rated value has been raised sharply since 1994.

Residents pay their tax on this notional income by having it added to their other income as if it were more earnings. This means that they pay tax at their normal income tax rate. If their incomes are modest they will pay 15 per cent and if their incomes are high they will pay 30 or even 40 per cent.

The non-resident is taxed always at the flat rate of 25 per cent on any income arising in Spain. Do not confuse this tax of 25 per cent on earnings with the capital gains tax of 35 per cent, which applies to profits from the sale of assets, such as a house or shares in a company.

If a non-resident husband and wife own a villa which has a *valor catastral* of 20 million pesetas and a real value of 30 million pesetas, we find that the Spanish Tax Agency imputes to them separately an ownership of 10 million pesetas each, half of the *valor catastral*.

We then calculate that 2 per cent of 10 million is 200,000 pesetas of imaginary income. Taxed at 25 per cent, this gives a bill of 50,000 pesetas. Add to that the 30,000 pesetas of Spanish wealth tax (see below) and you get a total of 80,000 pesetas due to the Spanish tax man from each of the co-owning spouses, or 160,000 pesetas total from both spouses. This is in addition to your annual real estate tax. (See below)

If we imagine that your annual real estate tax, IBI, on the villa is 40,000 pesetas, this means that it will cost you 200,000 pesetas a year in Spanish taxes simply to own the place.

Remember that non-residents using Form 214 can declare at any time during the year. Keep in mind that, if you own two properties in Spain, you cannot use Form 214 and must declare on Form 714 for wealth tax and Form 210 for imputed income tax, and you must declare in the period between May 1 and June 20. If you own two properties, you are still required to name an official *representante fiscal,* a tax representative in Spain.

If you fail to name a representative, you can be fined from 25,000 pesetas to one million pesetas.

One owner who applied for Form 214 was annoyed to discover that he was not eligible because he had purchased his garage separately from his house. Because he has two separate title deeds, he must fill out the standard forms, declare in the regular time period and name an official tax representative.

## 2. "Wealth Tax"

In addition to his income tax the Spanish resident — and non-resident property owner — is liable for Spain's tax on

THE SPANISH PROPERTY GUIDE

capital assets — *patrimonio* tax. The name "wealth tax" may not sound like proper legal terminology, but it is an adequate translation of the Spanish name, as it's exactly that: a tax on all your assets and property; your total wealth. Do not be alarmed, however.

In Spanish, the name is *impuesto extraordinario sobre el patrimonio,* the extraordinary tax on assets. This tax started in 1978 as a special measure to force many Spanish citizens who had been hiding their wealth, especially property, to bring these assets into the open.

Hacienda placed a very small tax on these assets, amounting to only .002, that is two-tenths of one per cent, or two-thousandths of the taxable base, up to assets of 27,808,000 pesetas. After that, the rate goes up as assets go up.

The idea was that anyone who did not then declare his assets in 1978 would be in violation and subject to fines. Further, any difference between assets declared at that time and such assets as later came to light would be treated as income for that year and taxed as such, at the much higher income tax rate, of course, going as high as 48 per cent.

The "extraordinary" tax worked more or less as projected, and many formerly hidden assets came to light. However, the State found it a good means of keeping track of people's wealth, so they have not yet discontinued it and it has become all-too ordinary and normal.

In our example above, we assigned half of the value of a house with a rated value of 20 million pesetas to each spouse, meaning that each half-owner would be subject to tax of 20,000 pesetas per year, at .002, or two-thousandths, of 10 million pesetas. In fact, the tax will almost certainly be higher, because it is not based on the rated value, but on the real sale value declared in the contract, which is almost always higher than the *valor catastral.*

In our example above, the sale value of the property was 30 million pesetas. Two-tenths of one per cent of this is 60,000 pesetas, or 30,000 pesetas for each of the husband and wife half-owners. (See below for more details)

You declare for this tax when you declare for your income tax, on the simplified Form 214 if you are a non-resident with only one property or on the separate Form 714.

But watch out. Changes are coming.

Since January 1, 1997, the administration of the wealth tax has been handed over from the central government in Madrid to each of the individual autonomous regions, like Andalusia and Valencia. This means that each region's taxpayers have to deal with their own separate system. If the regions decide to change the basics, taxpayers will have different exemptions and pay at different rates in each region. If the regional governments do not enact specific changes, the system will continue as it is, even though the regions will collect the tax and not the central government.

### Patrimonio Tax Rates - 2000

| Tax Base | Tax Payable | Rate Band To: | Marginal Rate % |
|---|---|---|---|
| 0 | 0 | 27,808,000 | 0.20 |
| 27,808,000 | 55,616 | 27,807,000 | 0.30 |
| 55,615,000 | 139,037 | 55,614,000 | 0.50 |
| 111,229,000 | 417,107 | 111,229,000 | 0.90 |
| 222,458,000 | 1,418,168 | 222,458,000 | 1.30 |
| 444,916,000 | 4,310,122 | 444,916,000 | 1.70 |
| 889,832,000 | 11,873,694 | 889,832,000 | 2.10 |
| 1,779,664,000 | 30,560,166 | excess | 2.50 |

Wealth tax affects residents and non-residents differently. A resident is required to declare his worldwide assets while the non-resident declares only his property and assets in Spain.

These taxable assets include anything he owns, not just real property. It can include bank deposits, stocks, shares, bonds, ownership of a business, gold bars under the mattress, automobiles, yachts, private aeroplanes, works of art unless they are owned by the maker, jewels, luxury fur coats or anything else that can be considered wealth. Your home furnishings are exempt unless they are valuable antiques. There are deductions available for debts against your business, mortgages on your property, and any tax of a similar nature paid in a foreign country.

The principal deduction for a resident of Spain is that he pays nothing on the first 18 million pesetas. A husband and wife each have an exemption of 18 million pesetas, and each must make an individual declaration. So, if they own together a property valued at almost 36 million pesetas, they each declare half the value, take their 18-million-peseta exemption, and have no *patrimonio* tax to pay.

As Spanish law views property as individually owned, for wealth tax purposes, this means that a husband and wife who own their home together, must each file a wealth tax declaration declaring 50 per cent of the value as their property.

For most of us, our principal wealth is our home so most residents wind up paying nothing under this tax. In fact, of 14 million Spanish residents declaring for income tax, only 800,000 of them had to pay anything in *patrimonio* tax.

But, as you see from the chart, if you have worldwide assets of about a million pounds Sterling, that is, over 250 million pesetas and you are a Spanish resident, you will have to pay wealth tax at more than 1.5 million pesetas each year.

## Non-Resident Must Pay

A non-resident who owns property in Spain, however little, will also have to pay something, because none of the exemptions above apply to non-residents. This is to ensure that the non-resident pays something each year towards the State's protection of his dwelling, such as police and fire departments. It is assumed that the resident is paying other taxes in Spain, such as income tax, and is entitled to a little relief in this area. The non-resident, however, is taxed only on his assets located in Spain.

## Wealth Tax Is Based...
### on Real Value of Property

Non-residents who own holiday property in Spain — and there are more than a million of them — are required to pay both *patrimonio* tax and Spanish income tax, because two per cent of the value of their property is attributed to them as a sort of notional income, on which they are charged income tax, just as if they had actually received the money.

If their *valor catastral* has been sharply raised since 1994, they will be rated at only 1.1 per cent, so their tax should not increase much even if their assessed value has gone up.

Until mid-1994 these non-resident property owners had to present Form 714 to declare for wealth tax and Form 210 to declare for non-resident income tax. A married couple with both names on the property title had to present a set of forms for each partner, totalling four. Further, they had to present the forms in the May 1 - June 20 tax period, with no allowance for being absent from Spain at that time. No wonder they needed a tax representative, a *representante fiscal,* to handle the business for them. People who own more than one property, including residents this time, must continue to go through this process.

Even when Spain dropped the requirement to appoint an official tax representative for owners of only one property, most non-residents continued to use their services.

But these million or more non-resident owners of only one property in Spain can now use the easy Form 214 to declare both taxes on one sheet of paper. Even better, they can present the form at any time during the year. Husbands and wives continue to need separate forms, however, if both names are on the property's *escritura.* This means that each spouse owns half the property, so each must make a separate declaration.

You can go directly to your local *Agencia Tributaria* office and make your declaration. Take both your IBI real estate tax receipt (see below) and your *escritura* because your wealth tax will be calculated on the basis of whichever value is higher, the assessed value —*valor catastral* — given on your IBI receipt or the declared purchase price shown on your *escritura*. This real value is almost always the base of your *patrimonio* tax.

A third value may even be used, such as the amount set by Hacienda for inheritance tax. This could happen when a very old property with a low valuation is transferred. The tax man will not accept the out-of-date valuation and will assign a new value closer to real market prices.

Your non-resident property owner's imputed income tax will, however, be based on the *valor catastral*.

## Raised valor catastral

In fact, Hacienda has been sharply raising the catastral values of many properties all over Spain. There is a sort of good news for those property owners who have found their assessed values suddenly raised to near market levels.

If this increase happened since 1994 under the revised regulations, Hacienda will apply only 1.1 per cent of this value, instead of 2 per cent, as imputed income for tax purposes. This applies to both residents and non-residents. This lower rate will not apply to those whose evaluations have been raised only slightly in line with normal yearly increases for inflation, so you will have to ask at Hacienda if the 1.1 per cent figure applies in your case.

Furthermore, starting in 1998, as Hacienda continued its upward revision of the assessed values, especially in Almeria and Valencia, a new system has been put into effect. When the *valor catastral* is sharply raised, the increase is not completely applied the first year. Instead, it will be spread out over 10 years, with a 10 per cent increase each year. At the end of the 10 years, the values will be revised again.

This system has the advantage that the property owner knows exactly what his valuation will be each year, instead of receiving it as an unpleasant surprise.So, how much will this *patrimonio* tax wind up costing you?

Let's suppose that, as in our example above, your villa has a contract price of 30 million pesetas and that this is higher than your *valor catastral,* which is 20 million pesetas, so the contract price is the value to declare. Half of this amount is attributed to each spouse, so we start with a tax base of 15 million pesetas for each partner.

For *patrimonio* tax, the rate of two-tenths of one per cent — .002 — is applied to values up to 27 million pesetas. Above that, the percentage goes up slightly. We apply the .002 to 15 million and we get a tax of 30,000 pesetas for each owner. If you do not own your Spanish property free and clear, you can deduct any outstanding debt from its value. That is, if you still owe 8 million pesetas on your mortgage, you subtract this from 30 million and pay tax on 22 million. Until 1994, non-residents were permitted no deductions at all on their Spanish property, so this is a welcome change.

Keep in mind that the non-resident has no exemption like the resident's 18 million pesetas, so they have to pay from the first peseta.

To continue our example, we now have our married couple owning the house each paying 50,000 pesetas imputed income tax based on the rated value of 20 million pesetas plus 30,000 pesetas wealth tax based on real value 30 million pesetas, that is, 80,000 pesetas each, for a total of 160,000 pesetas per year, every year.

In addition to this they pay the annual real estate tax.

## 3. Annual Real Estate Tax

The annual real estate tax on your Spanish property must also be paid. This tax, based on your *valor catastral,* can vary widely from town to town for the same type of property because it is a municipal tax. You can expect to pay much more for a townhouse in Marbella than you would pay for the same accommodation in an inland provincial town. If you live in a typical village house set back from the coast, your annual real estate tax could be as little as 10,000 pesetas. If you have a well-positioned villa on a large lot you could pay as much as 300,000 pesetas.

This real estate tax is called the IBI, the *Impuesto sobre Bienes Inmuebles*. For the year 2000, property owners will find their IBI raised 2 per cent across the board as a result of inflation.

If you are a non-resident, the best solution for you is to have the tax *domiciliado* in your bank. This is a standing order to the bank to pay the tax — and you can include any other municipal charges as well. You obtain a form at the bank which authorizes them to pay the tax bill, and you deposit a copy of the form with your *ayuntamiento*. This tells them where to send the bill. You are thus assured that your taxes are paid when they are due, the same as the telephone, water and electric bills.

If you prefer to pay the bill in person, you will have to go to your Town Hall and pay it each year. Some towns offer a discount for early payment, so be sure to ask.

In addition to the *valor catastral,* the assessed value of your property for tax purposes, the IBI also lists your *referencia catastral* number, which will locate your property at the *Catastro* office, along with its officially measured dimensions. This can be important in buying and selling property because sometimes the physical description does not agree with the description given in the property title.

For example, the property title might refer only to the land, while the catastral description shows that there is a large villa standing on the property. The *referencia catastral* number is now necessary when property sales are made.

To round off our example of what it will cost you each and every year simply to own your Spanish property, let's suppose that our villa at 30 million pesetas sits on a modest plot, and attracts an IBI each year of 40,000 pesetas. Added to the 160,000 pesetas of wealth tax and property owners' income tax, this gives a total annual expense of 200,000 pesetas in taxes on ownership.

If you think that you can simply forget about these three taxes because you are not a Spanish resident and someday will sell your home in the sun anyway, think again. The

Spanish tax agency, Hacienda, will check the books at the time of the property sale, and they will be holding a deposit of 5 per cent of your total sale price against your capital gains liability, as well as the income tax and wealth tax obligations for the last five years. You will also be required to present the current real estate tax receipt, the IBI, when you sign the sale contract.

## Community Charges

The fees charged annually by your Community of Property Owners, to pay for your share of maintaining the community property, are not taxes of course, but they need to be factored into your totals when you are calculating the annual running costs of your Spanish property. These fees might be as little as 50,000 pesetas a year for a small flat or more like 500,000 pesetas a year for a luxury villa on an elegant estate in Marbella.

## Rental or Business Income
### Form 210

If you spend less than 183 days in Spain and do not hold a residence permit, you are liable only for income tax on any of your income which arises in Spain. That is, you might let your flat in Spain and get income from this, on which you must pay Spanish income tax. In fact, in this particular case, you should be paying to Hacienda 25 per cent of your rentals received as a withholding tax in the first place, even if the total of such rentals does not exceed 1.2 million pesetas in one year. This is because you are presumed to be in business — the business of letting your flat — and this is a different class of tax from income tax on your earnings from work.

So all non-residents who are making money by renting out their Spanish property are subject to tax on this income arising in Spain. They are required to declare their Spanish income on Form 210. They are supposed to declare within 30 days of receiving the income, but they can apply to make their declarations quarterly to save paperwork.

If you are a non-resident but you own and operate a business in Spain, such as a restaurant, or a bar, or a cement factory, you are also liable for Spanish tax on your profits.

You would also use Form 210 if you are a rock music star and you give a series of concerts in Spain. You declare your earnings within 30 days and you are taxed at the same 25 per cent. That is, if you were paid 10 million pesetas for your performance, you would have to pay 2.5 million pesetas to the Spanish tax man.

## Your Fiscal Representative

The non-resident property owner of only one property is no longer required by Spanish law to name a fiscal representative who is resident in Spain. Those who own two or more properties must do so, however, under penalty of fines that can go as high as one million pesetas if he does not comply.

The fiscal representative assures the Spanish tax authorities that they can have a reliable contact inside Spain for the non-resident taxpayer.

Although most non-residents name their tax consultant or lawyer as their fiscal representative, it can be anyone, even a foreigner, as long as he is officially resident in Spain. Any *gestoría* or tax office has the simple forms necessary.

Spanish law states that the fiscal representative can be held responsible for the payment of taxes by his principal, which makes such representation sound dangerous. However, Hacienda has declared that they will not attempt to prosecute any representative unless he has received the money from his principal, and failed to use the money to pay the taxes due.

## Non-Resident's
### *Fiscal Identification Number*

If you are a non-resident property owner, you will have the above-mentioned taxes to pay and perhaps a fiscal representative to name. In order to pay these taxes, you must apply for a *número de identificación de extranjero,* a NIE, which is your Spanish tax identification number. Residents, of course, have a number as well, and Spaniards do, too.

In fact, you should apply for this number when you purchase your property. The number identifies you to the Spanish taxman and is required when you pay your taxes or have any dealings with Hacienda.

To obtain it, simply present yourself at the nearest police *comisaría* with a foreigners' department, along with a photocopy of the first pages of your passport. Fill in the form and wait a few weeks for your number to be assigned. You can also have your *gestoría* do this for you.

Then you will be registered with Hacienda's central computers just like the rest of us in today's electronically observed society.

## Capital Gains Tax
### on Sale of Property

Since January 1, 1989, Spain has applied a capital gains tax of 35 per cent on profits earned by non-residents who sell their Spanish assets. This profit can arise from the sale of property, a business, or shares in Spanish companies. A non-resident who sells his Spanish home at a profit is liable for this tax, based on the difference between what he paid originally and what he sold it for.

Residents and Spaniards of course are also liable for capital gains tax when they sell property at a profit, but it is calculated in a different way and the resident gets a couple of breaks that the non-resident does not have. For one, his capital gains tax has a top limit of 20 per cent.

## Over-65s Don't Pay

The good news for the new millennium is that an official resident of Spain 65 or over now pays nothing on profits realized from the sale of his principal dwelling. If it is a holiday home, the tax is still due.

In addition, there are reduction factors based on the length of time the property has been owned that can be applied to the sales transaction in order to reduce the amount of tax paid. In a confusing series of rapid changes, the Spanish tax authorities first allowed property sellers to deduct 5.26 per cent of their profit for each year of ownership, with no tax due after 20 years. Then they doubled that to 11.11 per cent per year, with no capital gains tax at all after 10 years of ownership, and then they removed the deduction entirely, as of December 31, 1996. They replaced this with an inflation correction factor — *coeficiente de actualización* — which is designed to make up for the effects of inflation. And some property sellers are stuck in the middle of the two systems, using a little of both. (See the beginning of this chapter for a summary). Let's see if we can make sense of the system, starting with the new inflation corrector.

### *Coeficiente de Actualización*

This is the new magic number. It is a percentage which you apply to your original acquisition price of the property, that is, what you paid for it. The factor raises that original price to the same level in today's inflated pesetas. As the inflation has been small in recent years, the percentage is small, but it helps because it is applied to the entire purchase price.

It works like this: If you bought a property for 20 million pesetas in 1996 and you sell it in 2000 for 30 million pesetas, you have a profit of 10 million pesetas. Now you look at the table and you see that, for a property bought in 1996 and sold in 2000, the coefficient is 1.08. Hacienda estimates that this will correct for the inflation between 1996 and 2000. Multiplying, you now have a corrected purchase price of 21,660,000 pesetas. This means that your taxable profit has been reduced from an even 10 million pesetas to 8,340,000 pesetas.

If you pay capital gains tax as a resident, maximum of 20 per cent, this means you would pay two million pesetas on a profit of 10 million pesetas, but only 1,668,000 pesetas on your corrected profit, a saving of 332,000 pesetas. This may not seem like a great saving to you, but, in our example, the seller has made quite a big profit in a very short time, so he must be taxed on it. If he had owned it for a longer time, he would have larger reductions.

This is the system applied to all property purchased since the beginning of 1995, with no other reductions available. It means that all persons who buy Spanish property today (really, since January 1, 1995) will be subject to pay some capital gains tax, and all non-resident sellers will be subject to the retention of five per cent paid directly to the Spanish Tax Agency when they sell their property.

### *Coeficiente de Actualización*
### Inflation Correction Table

| PURCHASE DATE | SALE 2000 |
|---|---|
| Until 1994 | 1.059 |
| 1995 | 1.119 |
| 1996 | 1.080 |
| 1997 | 1.059 |
| 1998 | 1.038 |
| 1999 | 1.020 |
| 2000 | 1 |

**Using the Table**

You see that, from 1995 onwards, the table gives a graduated set of percentages designed to bring the original purchase price of the property up to date in today's inflated pesetas.

You multiply the factor by your purchase price. That is, if you paid 10 million pesetas in 1996, you multiply by 1.080 and you get a value of 10,800,000 pesetas. If you sell in 2000 for 12 million pesetas, this means that, instead of paying tax on a profit of two million pesetas, you pay on 1,200,000 pesetas, a substantial reduction. For all years before 1995, you can apply the factor of 1.059. This is lower than it should be, but Hacienda knows that those who bought before 1995 will also have at least part of the reduction of 11.11 per cent per year that was applied formerly. See the example at the end of this section for a sample calculation for these "transitional" sellers, who must use part of both systems. Keep in mind that new tables will be published in 2001 and each year thereafter, depending on the current rate of inflation.

## Include Expenses

When you calculate your capital gains tax, you also get to include any officially registered expenses you had as a result of the purchase. This means that you can add to your original purchase price the amount of property transfer tax you paid at the time, at 6 per cent, or at 7.5 per cent if you bought a new property from a developer, thus paying IVA instead of transfer tax, along with expenses for notary, property registration, the *plus valía* tax if you as the buyer had to pay it, and lawyer. You need the official receipts for these payments in order to claim them.

So, if we suppose, as in our example above, that these expenses totalled one million pesetas on top of the 10 million you actually paid for the property. You get to add them in first, thus making your total acquisition cost 11 million pesetas, what you really had to pay out.

Then you apply your correction factor of 1.080 to 11 million pesetas and your new, corrected, price of acquiring the property becomes 11,880,000 pesetas. Your new tax base, which is your real profit, is then only 120,000 pesetas, on which you pay just 24,000 pesetas tax if you are a resident paying at 20 per cent, or just about 45,000 pesetas if you are a non-resident paying at 35 per cent. Your tax has been sharply cut by applying the correction factor and adding in the expenses.

Those non-residents who make big profits in a short time in today's fast-moving Spanish property market can face big capital gains tax bills, however.

## Break for Residents

In addition, an official resident of Spain who reinvests all of the proceeds of his house sale to purchase another Spanish home as his principal residence will get complete relief from this tax. If he uses only a portion of the total amount of his house sale, he will get a percentage of relief up to the amount reinvested.

One frequent situation is where an older couple sell their large villa, which they no longer need, and move into a smaller apartment, using the rest of their profits to improve their life style. If we suppose that the couple originally bought the villa for 20 million pesetas and sell it today for 30 million pesetas, they have a profit of 10 million pesetas.

If they buy a new flat for the whole of the 30 million pesetas selling price, they will have no Spanish capital gains tax to pay. But if they buy a small flat for 10 million pesetas, and keep the remaining 20 million in cash, they will have used only one-third of their sale proceeds to purchase a new principal residence. Thus, they get to deduct only one-third of their profits. One third of 10 million is 3,333,333 pesetas, so they subtract this from 10 million profit, leaving 6,666,666 pesetas to be taxed.

This will in fact be less because they can apply the correction factor, and, if they have owned their property for 10 years before December 31, 1996, they will have no capital gains tax to pay at all.

This remaining profit will be taxed as an *incremento de patrimonio,* a capital gain, as part of their Spanish income tax. If their income is modest and they pay Spanish income tax at a rate of 15 per cent or so, then they will pay capital gains tax at the same rate.

If their income is higher, they may be subject to Spanish income tax at rates of 30 or 40 per cent. However, they get another break here, as their capital gains tax is limited to a maximum of 20 per cent. Thus, they could never pay more than about 1.3 million pesetas on their 6.6 million pesetas of taxable profit. Formerly, the resident's capital gains tax could be even higher than the non-resident's 35 per cent, if the resident was in a high tax bracket, but government tax reductions in 1996 put on the cap of 20 per cent.

This limit applies to any sort of capital gain realized by a resident, whether he sells shares at a profit or anything else. It is not limited to property sales only.

Take professional advice in each case when you plan to sell your Spanish property, whether you are resident or non-resident.

Even 1.3 million pesetas seems like a nasty tax, but we have not yet applied any of the adjustments available for the amount of time you have owned the property. Almost nobody buys a house one day and sells it the next for a big profit.

Let's look again at the three possible situations listed at the beginning of this chapter.

If our elderly couple bought their house before 1987, more than 10 years passed before December 31, 1996, and so they have no capital gains tax to pay at all.

If they originally bought in 1995 or after, they can apply the new inflation correction factor as described above.

If they bought between 1987 and 1994, they are caught in the middle of the old and the new system, so they must apply some of each. First, they can apply the correction factor of 1.059 applied to purchases before 1995. Then they calculate their profit, and then they apply the reduction factor of 11.11 per cent per year, after the first two years of ownership, to their profit. See the example below for a calculation of this "transitional" type of sale.

So the new provision that residents over 65 selling their principal dwelling have no capital gains tax can come in awfully handy here. If you are over 65 and hold a residence permit, you can simply skip this section entirely.

### Non-Resident Pays 35%

The Spanish tax man is harder on the non-resident. Where the resident's capital gains tax is limited to 20 per cent, and can even be less, the non-resident must pay at the rate of 35 per cent, whether his profit is large or small.

If you, as a non-resident, bought your holiday flat for 10 million pesetas and now sell it for 20 million, you have a profit of 10 million. At 35 per cent, your tax is 3.5 million, a nasty bite, so the reductions will be even more important to you as a non-resident.

## Usufruct

Another capital gains change provides benefits for those elderly persons who use the "inherit from yourself" schemes in which you sell your house but retain the right to live in it until your death.

So, a person 65 or older who contracts with a company to sell his principal residence in exchange for the lifetime right to inhabit the dwelling, along with a monthly payment, will not be taxed on any capital gain involved. This makes such deals to turn your home ownership into lifetime income more attractive for older persons of modest means. The right to inhabit the property is called a *usufructo*. This usufruct is also used to avoid, quite legally, one round of Spanish inheritance tax. The parents will purchase their Spanish property in the names of their children, while reserving for themselves the right to inhabit the flat or house for as long as they live. Thus, when they die, the children simply take full possession of the property without having to inherit it, as it is already in their names.

## Five Per Cent Tax Deposit
### On Non-Resident Sale

In order to make sure that the non-resident property seller actually pays his capital gains tax instead of just taking the money and running, on January 1, 1992, Spain closed yet another loophole in its tax net by putting into force a requirement that 10 per cent of the declared purchase price of a property sale must be deposited with Hacienda when property is sold by a non-resident. In 1996 they lowered this deposit to five per cent.

For years before that, any non-resident who sold his Spanish property simply put a clause in the contract that the purchaser was responsible for any taxes or fees arising from the sale, and disappeared.

Spanish lawyers often "forgot" to advise their non-resident clients that they were liable for Spain's 35 per cent tax on capital gains, even with such a clause in the contract, as the tax applies only to the individual who makes the capital gain.

So many non-resident sellers conveniently evaded the tax and became so hard to find that Spain decided to end the situation.

### Form 211

Now anyone who purchases a Spanish property from a non-resident must be warned by the Notary that he is required by law to fill in Form 211, available from Hacienda offices, and deposit five per cent of the full purchase price with the tax ministry as a deposit against any tax due.

This means that, if you purchase a property from a non-resident for 20 million pesetas, you must file the form and deposit one million pesetas. The buyer receives only 95 per cent of the agreed price.

### *Ley de Tasas*

If the buyer and seller are disposed to declare a very low value on the sale for tax purposes, remember that the *Ley de Tasas,* the law on public fees, now makes it an offence to under-declare a contract. If Hacienda determines, by its own evaluation, that you have under-declared the value of the sale by more than 20 per cent, or two million pesetas, both parties can be heavily fined.

In you have any doubts about this, you can ask at the Hacienda evaluation office, called the *oficina liquidadora,* and they will tell you what they consider a fair market price for any registered property. They have tables and charts and are perfectly well aware of the going price for property in any region. Dozens of low declarers have learned to their sorrow that Big Brother really is watching you. They receive a notice that their declared price on the sale is too low, and a bill for the additional tax they must pay.

This five per cent deposit is no bother, really, to the purchaser, as he should pay no more than the agreed price. It's only that he must pay five per cent of it directly to the taxman in the name of the seller.

If he fails to do this, even after being warned by the Spanish Notary, the tax agency can put a lien on his new property to recover the amount.

The seller, when he settles up his tax liabilities on the purchase, will either have to pay more to Hacienda or will get a refund, depending on the amount of his profit.

But what about people who sell at a loss? Do they have to make this deposit also? Yes, they do. The deposit is not based on the real profit of the sale, but on the total amount. If you bought a property for 20 million pesetas a few years ago and you now sell it for 15 million, you have a loss of five million pesetas. Even so, the 750,000 pesetas, representing five per cent of the total sales price, must be deposited with the taxman.

The unfortunate seller can then claim a refund from Hacienda, and they promise to act within two months to return the money, as no tax is due.

That's their promise. Reports from recent sellers indicate that the tax man is taking up to a year to return such overpayment.

## LETTERS

The following two letters have been received from puzzled tax payers. We hope the answers will help you to see how the capital gains tax picture works in real life.

**COULD YOU PLEASE** clarify the situation regarding Spanish capital gains tax on the sale of property and the five per cent retention paid to directly to Spain's Tax Agency when a non-resident sells his property?

I have understood that both residents and non-residents were allowed to reduce any profit from a property sale by 11.11 per cent per year of ownership, after the first two years, and that, after 10 years of ownership, there was no capital gains tax at all, for both residents and non-residents.

However, according to my tax consultant, and the new tax form 212, this reduction applies only up to December

31, 1996. After that date, you can apply a series of coefficients to correct for inflation, but these factors do not compensate totally for the loss of the years of 11.11 per cent discount.

I am also confused by the percentages given in the table on the new tax form 212. For a property owned three years, thus giving a right to one year of reduction, it says to apply a percentage of 88.89 per cent to your profit. Is this the same as taking 11.11 per cent away?

Now, if the years for the reduction factor of 11.11 per cent can only be counted up until December 31, 1996, this means that anyone selling now, in 2000 is going to lose some years of reductions. If they bought in 1993, for example, which is seven years ago, they will pay at a rate of 77.78 per cent, getting only two years' worth of reductions. Under the old system they would have got five years.

Presumably, the new *coeficiente de actualización*, which you apply to bring your original purchase price up to date is intended to correct this, but it does not fully compensate for the loss of the year of discount.

Furthermore, according to a Spanish Notary we consulted, even a property purchased in 1987 will be subject to some capital gains tax and also to the deposit of five per cent, even though 13 years have passed since its purchase. This is because the 10 years required for exemption from capital gains tax must have passed before December 31, 1996. So, those who bought in 1987 have only the reduction factor available to them before Dec. 31, 1996. This means, after taking away the first two years which don't count, they have seven years of reduction, meaning they must pay tax on about 20 per cent of their profits instead of being totally free.

Does this mean that anyone who bought his Spanish property after January 1, 1987, will never, ever be exempt from having to have the five per cent deducted from the sales price of his property? That's how it looks, if the ten years must have passed before December 31, 1996.

—S.J. (Alhaurin, Málaga)

**YOU ARE QUITE RIGHT**. Spain's new tax laws are bad news for property sellers, and buyers as well.

The changes are not really so new, as they date from 1996, but they are just beginning to show their effects as more property sellers become subject to capital gains tax. Property buyers today, just as you note, will never, ever, be able to escape the deposit of five per cent, if they are non-residents, and they will always, always, have to pay a substantial Spanish capital gains tax, both for residents and non-residents.

That is "never" and "always" until they change the law again.

Residents, unless they invest all of the proceeds of their sale in a new principal residence in Spain, will pay capital gains tax at a maximum of 20 per cent. This can be less, as it is calculated as part of the resident's Spanish income tax, but it is limited to a maximum of 20 per cent. Non-residents pay at a flat rate of 35 per cent, regardless of how big or small their profit.

To answer your main question, yes, you are subject to Spanish capital gains tax and the deposit of five per cent even though you have owned your property for 13 years. Yes, it is true that you must have owned your property for ten years before December 31, 1996, in order to be free of Spanish capital gains tax. Yes, it is true that nobody who bought his Spanish property after January 1, 1987, will ever be free of capital gains tax.

**No More Reductions**

Let's note again the three possibilities for house sellers.

1.  No one who buys property in Spain today, since December 31, 1996, will be entitled to any reductions of 11.11 per cent year.

2.  Those who bought before 1987 will have their full 10 years, with the cutoff point being December 31, 1996.

3.  Those who bought in 1987 or after, will have the number of years of reduction cut off at December 31, 1996. As you note, a person who bought in 1987, has then, a nine-year period, to 1996. After taking off the first two years,

this seller has seven years worth of 11.11 reductions, total 77.77 per cent off their profit. So, they pay Spanish capital gains tax on only 22 per cent of their profit, but under the old system they would have been completely exempt.

If you bought your property in 1990, you would have four years of reduction, after you subtracted the first two years. If you bought at the beginning of 1995, you have no reduction at all, because of the initial two-year period.

So, what happens after 1996? This is where the new system, not nearly as favourable to capital gains, comes into play. As you said, it is based on the *coeficiente de actualización,* a factor that is applied to your original purchase price to bring it up to date in today's inflated pesetas.

Any purchase made before 1994 has a factor of 1.059 applied to it. This means that, if you bought for five million, your price is brought up to date at 5,294,000 pesetas at today's value.

So, if you sell today for, say, seven million, your profit is reduced from two million to 1,806,000, correcting for inflation. Then you have two years of reductions, a total of 22.22 per cent, which brings your taxable profit down to about 1.4 million. At a non-resident tax of 35 per cent, you pay about 500,000 pesetas tax. If your five per cent deposit is 350,000 pesetas, you will still owe the Spanish tax man 150,000 pesetas, declaring on your Form 212.

Are you still with us? And keep in mind that we have omitted from our calculations the costs associated with your original purchase, which are also deductible. These include the transfer tax you paid at the time, the notary and registration fees, the lawyer and gestoría, the *plus valía* tax, and the estate agent's fee. All these can be added on to your original purchase price, thus reducing your final profit. And also of course, any expansion or improvements you have made to your property, such as an added bedroom or a new swimming pool.

Finally, you are right when you suggest that the tables given on the back of the new Form 212 simply express the

11.11 per cent per year reduction from the other end. Instead of noting that you take off 11.11 per cent for the first year and 22.22 per cent for the second year and so on, the tables state that, for the first year of the reduction, you pay 88.89 per cent and so on.

## Everyone Will Pay

Summing up for the future, the change in laws means that everyone will pay capital gains tax. The law applies to any capital gain, such as profits from selling shares, as well as to property sales.

The *coeficiente de actualización* only has the effect of correcting the inflationary rise in values. Because inflation is now low, the factor is small. You apply it to your original purchase price to make it the same value as today's pesetas, or euros as it will be. Then you pay tax on your entire profit from the sale.

The news is not all bad, however. Because this updating coefficient is applied to the full amount of your original purchase price, it has a strong multiplying effect, and you should not wind up paying much more tax than you would have under the old system. In some cases, it will even be less tax.

## What happens to the tax reduction when the land was bought first and the house built years later?

WHAT HAPPENS TO the capital gains tax situation when you sell a house that was built some years after you bought the land? That is, we purchased the plot of land in 1984 but we did not build the house until 1990, when we made our *declaración de obra nueva,* the declaration of new work, all in correct form. Now we are selling the house and land. According to advice we received from the Spanish Tax Agency, we can express the land and the house separately in our sales contract, assigning a value to each of them. This means, in our case, that any amount of profit assigned to the land alone would be free of capital gains tax, as we have owned it for 10 years before December 31, 1996. The amount of profit assigned to the house itself would be subject to some capital gains tax because we would have only four years of 11.11 per cent reductions, from 1992 (subtracting the first two years of ownership) to 1996, when the 11.11 reduction was cut off.

Nevertheless, two Spanish Notaries with whom we spoke were reluctant to do this and we are not sure about why. Any comment would be appreciated.

PJ. Estepona

**I AM NOT SURE** about why, either. Yes, your situation is fairly frequent, where the land is purchased first and a house not built until some years later.

It is indeed, as the tax agency advised you, an accepted practice in such a case to express the values of the land and the building on it separately in the contract, declaring that the land is sold at such a price and the building at such a price.

For capital gains, you would note the two operations as separate on your 212 form, one part noting that the land was exempt from capital gains because you had owned it for more than ten years before December 31, 1996, and the other part calculating the amount of tax due on the amount of the sale corresponding to the house.

Your purchaser would file his own form depositing five per cent of the amount corresponding to the house. If this was more than your tax, you could claim any overpayment back from Hacienda on your own 212. If you had to pay more, you would pay when you filed the form.

Your Notary might have been reluctant to make out your contract in this way because this type of declaration is often subject to fraud, in that the seller assigns an extremely high value to the land (exempt from tax) and a very low value to the house, thus evading part of his taxes.

You can be sure that Hacienda will examine such a declaration very carefully, so you want to assign the correct values.

## Special Tax on Offshore Companies

During the property boom of the 1980's thousands of luxury homes on the Spanish Costas were sold on the basis of ownership through a non-resident company. Many of these offshore companies are located in the so-called "tax havens" where little or no local taxes are charged and the names of the owners are confidential. On the Costa del Sol, entire urbanizations were marketed with Gibraltar companies already formed to own the property. The buyer purchased the Gibraltar company, in Gibraltar, and his real name never appeared on any Spanish documents, only the name of the Gibraltar company.

Estimates are that at least 12,000 companies exist, in Gibraltar alone, without mentioning other offshore tax havens, for the sole purpose of owning property in Spain. These companies were created, quite legally, as a means to slide around a number of Spanish taxes while concealing the identity of the true owners of the property.

Other non-resident companies are located in European countries where they are subject to tax like any other company, including tax on their assets in Spain.

There is nothing incorrect about this sort of operation, and it means that all Spanish transfer taxes — which can amount to 10 per cent of the price — are bypassed when property owned by such companies changes hands. This is because only the offshore company is bought and sold, a transaction which takes place outside of Spain. As far as the Spanish government is concerned, the property is still owned by the same company, and no change has taken place, so no tax is due. This offshore company ownership also avoids Spanish inheritance tax. The company is not registered in Spain, even though it possesses an asset here, so no Spanish inheritance tax is charged when the company is bequeathed to its inheritor, who then continues to own the company through Gibraltar, the Channel Islands, or some other country.

This is all perfectly legal. Nevertheless, it is not quite cricket and finally the loss of tax revenue irritated the Spanish authorities so much that they enacted a special tax on offshore companies. They are not the first to do so. In fact they were just about the last country in Europe to permit these operations.

## Special Tax Is 3%

Spain first placed a tax of 5 per cent of the assessed value of the property every year, for properties where the owners refused to reveal their details to the Spanish tax authorities, while granting exemptions to companies that revealed all details of the real owners. Then, as of January 1, 1996, this special tax on offshore companies was lowered to 3 per cent of the *valor catastral*. This means that, if your property is valued at 10 million pesetas (with a real market value of perhaps 20 million), your annual tax is 300,000 pesetas, very stiff indeed.

For companies registered in Gibraltar or other tax havens around the world, there are absolutely no exemptions. From 1992 to 1995, the tax was charged at 5 per cent but such offshore companies could claim exemption by revealing all their details to the Spanish tax office. This system proved not to be effective so it has been replaced and tax haven companies cannot claim exemption. Spain's tax ministry has a list of jurisdictions regarded as "tax havens".

However, when both the company and its real owners are fiscal residents of "normal" countries which have taxation treaties with Spain, the company can claim exemption from the new tax of 3 per cent by revealing all details of the owners and presenting certification that the company pays its taxes in its country of fiscal registration.

The new law is designed to crack down on those persons taking advantage of secrecy provisions in tax havens while permitting perfectly legitimate companies to continue to own property in Spain as long as they pay their taxes at home.

This leaves perfectly legitimate owners of tax haven companies, however, in the position of either having to pay the stiff tax or divest themselves of their companies.

If they "sell" the property to themselves as the new individual owners, this operation attracts tax at about 10 per cent of the total operation, just like any normal property sale. Some lawyers have been able to wind up the Gibraltar company and distribute its assets to the owners, under a small business tax of one per cent, plus a few other charges that bring the total expense to about three per cent.

This leaves you as an individual owning your home in Spain, just like almost everyone else, and subject to all the usual Spanish taxes we have discussed.

Another possibility, if you really prefer company ownership, is to transfer your Gibraltar company's assets, the property, to a newly-constituted Spanish company. Then your Spanish company will be taxed at Spanish company rates on its assets, the property, and its rental value. In addition, you have legal costs in forming and operating the company, even if it does not do any business.

A third option would be to transfer the offshore company to a company located in a "normal" country, where the new company will be subject to tax under the laws of that country.

Companies located in countries which have double taxation agreements with Spain and these agreements include a clause for the exchange of information, will be able to continue to obtain exemption from the tax by providing certification from the tax authorities in their home countries, but they must make new application for this exemption.

As the tax is based on the *valor catastral,* the assessed value, paying the tax might be a viable option in situations where this value is much lower than the real value. There are still cases where properties that are worth 30 million pesetas on the market have an assessed value of seven or eight million pesetas.

In such cases and where the individual has special need for confidentiality in his ownership, it could be a possible course of action. Be warned, however, that Spain continues its process of raising the *valor catastral* towards normal market prices. Furthermore, European Union commissions are now studying the possibility of stricter controls over tax havens as part of the EU campaign to discover the hiding places of black money obtained through various types of illegal operations.

Each case will need individual study and some careful planning.

# Spanish Property
# Tax Forms
# 211– 214

## FORM 211

This is the form used for declaring your deposit of five per cent paid to Spain's Tax Agency when you purchase property from a non-resident.

**Datos del Adquirente:** Here you enter name, address and details of the buyer, including his NIE, his tax identification number in Spain, even though Form says NIF. If you have Hacienda stickers, *etiquetas,* you can use these instead.

**Devengo:** Date of the sale.

**Datos del Transmitente:** Enter details of the non-resident seller. Where it says: "Clave Pais", a separate sheet gives you a three-digit number code for every country.

**Representante:** If you have a fiscal representative in Spain (not required if you own only one property) you enter his details here.

**Descripción del Inmueble:** Description of the property, including the address, whether or not it is being transmitted through a private document or a public document signed before a Notary, and, if so, the Notary and his registration number of the contract. Finally, enter the Catastral Reference number.

**Liquidación:** The liquidation is the calculation of the amount. Here you enter the declared price of the sale and calculate five per cent of it.

**Adquirente:** Buyer signs, with date.

**Ingreso:** Enter your form of payment, whether in cash or by certified cheque made out to "Tesoro Publico".

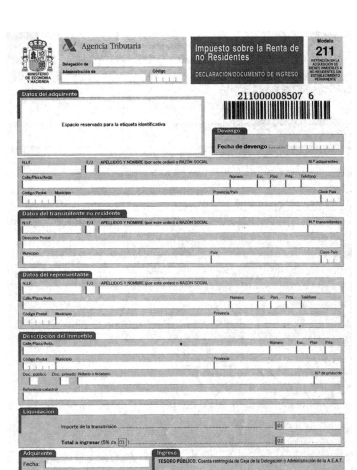

**MINISTERIO DE ECONOMIA Y HACIENDA**

Agencia Tributaria

Delegación de
Administración de          Código

**Impuesto sobre la Renta de no Residentes**

DECLARACIÓN/DOCUMENTO DE INGRESO

**Modelo 211**

RETENCIÓN EN LA ADQUISICIÓN DE BIENES INMUEBLES A NO RESIDENTES SIN ESTABLECIMIENTO PERMANENTE

**Datos del adquirente**

Espacio reservado para la etiqueta identificativa

211000008507 6

**Devengo**

Fecha de devengo .........

N.I.F.          F/J     APELLIDOS Y NOMBRE (por este orden) o RAZÓN SOCIAL          N.º adquirentes

Calle/Plaza/Avda.          Número     Esc.   Piso   Prta.   Teléfono

Código Postal     Municipio          Provincia/País          Clave País

**Datos del transmitente no residente**

N.I.F.          F/J     APELLIDOS Y NOMBRE (por este orden) o RAZÓN SOCIAL          N.º transmitentes

Dirección Postal

Municipio          País          Clave País

**Datos del representante**

N.I.F.          F/J     APELLIDOS Y NOMBRE (por este orden) o RAZÓN SOCIAL

Calle/Plaza/Avda.          Número     Esc.   Piso   Prta.   Teléfono

Código Postal     Municipio          Provincia

**Descripción del inmueble**

Calle/Plaza/Avda.          Número     Esc.   Piso   Prta.

Código Postal     Municipio          Provincia

Doc. público   Doc. privado   Notario o fedatario          N.º de protocolo

Referencia catastral

**Liquidación**

Importe de la transmisión ...............................................................................     01

Total a ingresar (5% de 01 )...........................................................................     02

**Adquirente**

Fecha:

Firma:

**Ingreso**

TESORO PÚBLICO. Cuenta restringida de Caja de la Delegación o Administración de la A.E.A.T.

Forma de pago:   ☐ Dinero de curso legal   ☐ Cheque conformado y nominativo a favor del Tesoro Público

Importe: I

**Espacio reservado para la Administración**

Ejemplar para la Administración

## FORM 212

This is the form on which the non-resident declares his capital gain or loss when he sells his Spanish property. On this form the non-resident seller either applies for a refund, if the deposit of 5 per cent is greater than the tax, or makes an extra payment, if the deposit is less than the tax due.

**Contribuyente:** List your name and address and fiscal number, or, if you have them, affix one of your tax labels here. F/J is "F" for a person and "J" for a company. If spouses declare together, give percentage of ownership. "Codigo Extranjero" is for your tax number in your home country.

**Conyuge:** Fiscal number and name and percentage of ownership of the spouse.

**Representante:** If you have a Fiscal Representative in Spain, enter his details here.

**Adquirente:** List details of the buyer.

**Descripción:** Description of the property. Give the name of the Notary before whom the contract was signed and list his Protocol Number for the document.

**Liquidación:** Liquidation is the calculation of the tax on your capital gain. First, you must list the number of the Form 211 on which your buyer made his payment of the five per cent deposit. Then you enter in Box 1 the net price you received for the property, after you have deducted all your expenses involved in the sale. In Box 2 you enter your original cost of acquiring the property, adding in all your expenses at the time, such as taxes and legal fees. You apply the inflation correction factor at this point. See the text for examples of calculations. In Box 3 you enter the difference. If you bought your property before Dec. 31, 1994, you now apply the 11.11 per cent per year factor, as described in the text, in order to get your tax base, entered in Box 4. The second table is for any additions you have made to the property. Box 4 will then be your taxable base, entered again in Box 9. Your tax rate will be 35 per cent as a non-resident.

Enter total tax in Box 11. Subtract 5 per cent, shown in Box 13, and you have the "Cuota Diferencial", the amount you must either pay or claim back on the second sheet of Form 212 (Not shown).

## Agencia Tributaria

Delegación de
Administración de                    Código

### Impuesto sobre la Renta de no Residentes.
No residentes sin establecimiento permanente

**Modelo 212**
DECLARACIÓN
DE RENTAS DERIVADAS
DE TRANSMISIONES
DE BIENES INMUEBLES

MINISTERIO
DE ECONOMÍA
Y HACIENDA

### Contribuyente

Espacio reservado para la etiqueta identificativa

212000009816 0

### Devengo

Fecha de transmisión.........

| N.I.F. | F/J | APELLIDOS Y NOMBRE (por este orden) o RAZÓN SOCIAL | Cuota particip. % |

| Código extranjero | Dirección a efectos de notificación | | |

| Código Postal | Municipio | Provincia/País | Código País |

### Cónyuge

| N.I.F. | APELLIDOS Y NOMBRE | Cuota particip. Código País % |

### Representante

| N.I.F. | F/J | APELLIDOS Y NOMBRE (por este orden) o RAZÓN SOCIAL |

| Calle/Plaza/Avda. | Número | Esc. | Piso | Prta. | Teléfono |

| Código Postal | Municipio | Provincia |

### Adquirente

| N.I.F. | F/J | APELLIDOS Y NOMBRE (por este orden) o RAZÓN SOCIAL |

| Calle/Plaza/Avda. | Número | Esc. | Piso | Prta. |

| Código Postal | Municipio | Provincia/País | Código País |

### Descripción del inmueble

| Calle/Plaza/Avda. | Número | Esc. | Piso | Prta. |

| Código Postal | Municipio | Provincia |

Doc. público Doc. privado  Notario o fedatario                    Nº de protocolo

Referencia catastral

### Liquidación

Número de justificante del modelo 211 adjunto

| | Adquisición | | Mejora o 2ª adquisición | |
|---|---|---|---|---|
| Valor de transmisión ............ | 1 | | 5 | |
| Valor de adquisición (actualizado) ............ | 2 | | 6 | |
| Diferencia ............ | 3 | | 7 | |
| Ganancia ............ | 4 | | 8 | |
| Fecha de adquisición | Base imponible ......... | | 9 | |
| | Tipo gravamen ............... | 10 % | | |
| | Cuota íntegra .......... | | 11 | |
| Fecha de mejora o 2ª adquisición | Deducción por donativos | | 12 | |
| | Retención ............... | | 13 | |
| | Cuota diferencial ( 11 - 12 - 13 ). | 14 | | |

### Fecha y firma

Fecha:                    Firma:                    Firma:

COLEGIO DE REGISTRADORES DE LA PROPIEDAD

**Ejemplar para la Administración**

## FORM 213

This is the form on which you either declare and pay your annual tax of 3 per cent on the *valor catastral,* or rated value, of your Spanish property owned by a non-resident company, or on which you cite your non-resident company's exemption from the tax.

**Entidad Sujeta:** Either paste in your Tax Agency label, or fill in the details of the non-resident company. "Codigo Extranjero" is the tax number, if it has one, in the country of registration.

**Devengo:** Enter year for which tax is being paid.

**Representante:** If the company has a fiscal representative in Spain, enter his details here.

**Exenciones:** Companies which are exempt from the tax check the appropriate box here. If your company is not located in a tax haven, and it pays its taxes in a "normal" country, check Box 1, and so on. Only those non-resident companies located in tax havens must pay.

**Liquidación:** Your "Base Imponible" is the *valor catastral* of the property. Tax rate is 3 per cent of that value. If you have owned the property less than a full year, you will have a proportional reduction. Otherwise you pay the full tax. When a company has several owners, some of whom are entitled to exemption and others not, there is a reduction as well.

## NOTE:

**FORM 213** has two other sheets, one of them for listing all properties owned by the company, and another for entering the details of persons owning the company when exemption is requested because the company pays its taxes in a normal jurisdiction and discloses the names of its real owners.

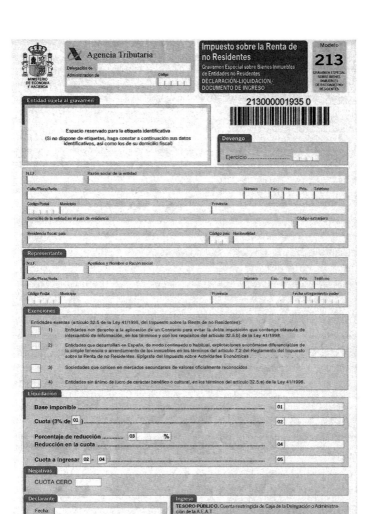

**Agencia Tributaria**

Delegación de
Administración de     Código

**MINISTERIO DE ECONOMIA Y HACIENDA**

**Impuesto sobre la Renta de no Residentes**

Gravamen Especial sobre Bienes Inmuebles de Entidades no Residentes

DECLARACION-LIQUIDACION/ DOCUMENTO DE INGRESO

Modelo

**213**

GRAVAMEN ESPECIAL SOBRE BIENES INMUEBLES DE ENTIDADES NO RESIDENTES

**Entidad sujeta al gravamen**

213000001935 0

Espacio reservado para la etiqueta identificativa
(Si no dispone de etiquetas, haga constar a continuación sus datos identificativos, así como los de su domicilio fiscal)

**Devengo**

Ejercicio.......................

N.I.F.     Razón social de la entidad

Calle/Plaza/Avda.     Número   Esc.   Piso   Prta.   Teléfono

Código Postal   Municipio     Provincia

Domicilio de la entidad en el país de residencia     Código extranjero

Residencia fiscal: país     Código país   Nacionalidad

**Representante**

N.I.F.     Apellidos y Nombre o Razón social

Calle/Plaza/Avda.     Número   Esc.   Piso   Prta.   Teléfono

Código Postal   Municipio     Provincia     Fecha otorgamiento poder

**Exenciones**

Entidades exentas (artículo 32.5 de la Ley 41/1998, del Impuesto sobre la Renta de no Residentes):

- 1) Entidades con derecho a la aplicación de un Convenio para evitar la doble imposición que contenga cláusula de intercambio de información, en los términos y con los requisitos del artículo 32.5.b) de la Ley 41/1998.
- 2) Entidades que desarrollen en España, de modo continuado o habitual, explotaciones económicas diferenciables de la simple tenencia o arrendamiento de los inmuebles en los términos del artículo 7.2 del Reglamento del Impuesto sobre la Renta de no Residentes. Epígrafe del Impuesto sobre Actividades Económicas .
- 3) Sociedades que coticen en mercados secundarios de valores oficialmente reconocidos.
- 4) Entidades sin ánimo de lucro de carácter benéfico o cultural, en los términos del artículo 32.5.e) de la Ley 41/1998.

**Liquidación**

Base imponible ...............................................................................................   01

Cuota (3% de 01 )..............................................................................................   02

Porcentaje de reducción ............. 03    %
Reducción en la cuota ......................................................................................   04

Cuota a ingresar 02 - 04 ...................................................................................   05

**Negativas**

CUOTA CERO

**Declarante**

Fecha:

Firma:

**Ingreso**

TESORO PÚBLICO. Cuenta restringida de Caja de la Delegación o Administración de la A.E.A.T

Forma de pago:   Dinero de curso legal   Cheque conformado y nominativo a favor del Tesoro Público

Importe:   I

Este documento no será válido sin la certificación mecánica o, en su defecto, firma autorizada

**Ejemplar para la Administración**

## FORM 214

This form is used by non-resident property owners to declare their Spanish capital assets tax, the *patrimonio*, also called wealth tax, and their non-resident property owner's imputed income tax, on the same one-page form. Residents are not subject to this tax on their principal dwelling.

**Contribuyente:** Stick on your Tax Agency printed label, or fill in the form with your name and address. Put your NIE where it says NIF.

**Devengo:** Enter the year.

**Liquidación Patrimonio:** For *patrimonio* tax, you enter the real declared price of the property in Box 1. Enter any debts against it, such as mortgages, in Box 2. The difference is your taxable base, Box 3. The percentages of the tax are given in a table on the back of the form and also in this book.

**Liquidación Renta:** To get Box 5, you apply to the *valor catastral* of the property either 2 per cent, or 1.1 per cent if your property has been sharply valued upward since 1994. Box 5 is your imaginary income. To this you apply 25 per cent, the non-resident income tax, to get Box 6, the amount of the tax.

**Total:** Add your two taxes together.

**Vivienda:** Enter details of the property, including the catastral reference number.

**Representante:** If you have a fiscal representative, list him here.

**Declarante:** Sign your name, with the date.

**Ingreso:** Enter your form of payment, cash or certified cheque.

MINISTERIO
DE ECONOMÍA
Y HACIENDA

**Agencia Tributaria**

Delegación de
Administración de                                    Código

**Impuesto sobre el Patrimonio y sobre la Renta de no Residentes**

No residentes sin establecimiento permanente

DECLARACIÓN-LIQUIDACIÓN /
DOCUMENTO DE INGRESO

Modelo
**214**

DECLARACIÓN
SIMPLIFICADA DE
NO RESIDENTES

**Contribuyente**

214000030296 4

Espacio reservado para la etiqueta identificativa

**Devengo**

Ejercicio....          Período ..... | 0 | A |

N.I.F.          APELLIDOS Y NOMBRE                                     Código extranjero

Dirección a efectos de notificaciones: nombre de la vía pública          Número   Esc.   Piso   Prta.   Teléfono

Código Postal   Municipio                                     Provincia/País

**Liquidación. Impuesto sobre el Patrimonio**

| | | |
|---|---|---|
| Valor ....................................................................... | 01 | |
| Deudas ................................................................... | 02 | |
| Base imponible y liquidable ................................. | 03 | |

Hasta
Resto                              al %
                    Suma
Cuota íntegra. Impuesto Patrimonio ................... | 04 |

**Liquidación. Impuesto sobre la Renta de no Residentes**

| | | |
|---|---|---|
| Base imponible ..................................................... | 05 | |
| Tipo de gravamen ............................ % | | |
| Cuota íntegra. Impuesto sobre la Renta de no Residentes ............ | 06 | |

**Total**

Total a ingresar ( 04 + 06 ) ...................................... | 07 |

**Vivienda**

Calle/Plaza/Avda.                                     Número   Esc.   Piso   Prta.

Código Postal   Municipio                                     Provincia

Referencia catastral

**Representante**

N.I.F.          APELLIDOS Y NOMBRE (por este orden) o RAZÓN SOCIAL

Calle/Plaza/Avda.                                     Número   Esc.   Piso   Prta.   Teléfono

Código Postal   Municipio                                     Provincia

**Declarante**                    **Ingreso**

Fecha:

Firma:

**TESORO PÚBLICO.** Cuenta restringida de Caja de la Delegación o Administración de la A.E.A.T.
Forma de pago:   ☐ Dinero de curso legal   ☐ Cheque conformado y nominativo a favor del Tesoro Público

Importe:  | I |

M 214 | 0 | 0 | Precio del juego: 60 Ptas./0,30 euros

**Ejemplar para la Administración**

# CHAPTER SIX

# CONTENTS

# Spanish Wills, Inheritance Tax

So, what happens to your Spanish property when you die? Can you bequeath it to your favourite nephew or are you bound by Spain's law of forcible inheritors? How much Spanish inheritance tax will your heirs have to pay? Should you make a Spanish will?

Let's answer two of these questions immediately.

1. Yes, you should make a Spanish will, disposing only of your property in Spain. It will save your inheritors time, trouble and money.

2. Yes, you, as a foreigner, can leave your Spanish property to whomever you choose, as long as the laws of your home country permit this.

3. Your inheritors will probably have to pay some Spanish inheritance tax, and we will see how much in the next section.

But let's take things in order.

## Spanish Inheritance Laws
### *Restrict Freedom*

Spanish inheritance laws restrict the testator's freedom to leave his property to anyone he pleases, in order to protect the family and provide for the children. It is almost impossible for a Spanish parent to make the classic threat that he will cut the no-good son out of his will. This is because Spanish law requires a parent to leave two-thirds of his estate to his children, even bypassing the surviving spouse.

In general, most people find that their ideas agree basically with what Spanish law provides as they wish to provide for their children, and they have no problem in making a Spanish will in accordance with those provisions.

First, let us establish just what the estate consists of when a person dies.

In Spanish law, a surviving spouse keeps all assets acquired before the marriage, half of the goods acquired during marriage, and all personal gifts or inheritances which have come directly to this spouse. Assuming that most of the couple's assets were acquired during their marriage, this means that about half of their assets do not really form part of the deceased person's estate. Half of the property continues to belong to the surviving spouse. This is particularly true of real estate. If the names of husband and wife both figure on the title deed of the property, each has one half of the ownership. Thus, when one dies, only half of the Spanish property is transmitted. The living spouse continues to own his or her half, with his or her name on the title deed.

Of the rest of the assets, only one-third can be freely disposed of, under the law of *herederos forzosos,* or obligatory heirs. When a person dies leaving children, the estate is divided into three equal parts. One of these thirds must be left to surviving issue in equal parts. Another third must also be left to the children, but the testator may decide how to divide it. That is, he can choose to leave all of this third to only one of his children or grandchildren. A surviving spouse has a life interest in this third; that is, if it should consist of a house or a piece of property, the child who inherits it cannot dispose of it freely until his surviving parent dies, because the surviving parent holds an usufruct over the property. The final third of the estate can be freely willed to anyone the testator chooses.

If a foreign resident dies in Spain without a will, his estate in Spain will be distributed according to the Spanish laws of succession.

### *Example:*

Suppose that a husband and father dies, leaving a widow and three children. The only property is the house. The widow continues to own half the house, because her name is on the title deed as half-owner. The other half of the house constitutes the estate. This is divided equally among the three children. When the estate is settled, each child will have one-third title to half of the house, meaning that each one now owns one-sixth of the house, and the title deed has four names on it, the widow and each of the three children. The widow also holds an usufruct — *usufructo* — on the children's share. This means she can use their half of the property until she dies, as well as her own half. They must all agree and sign the deed if the house is to be sold.

It is this provision of the inheritance law that causes the situation frequently seen in the Spanish countryside and villages, where six brothers are part-owners of a finca or a pueblo house.

Dying without a will can cause time-consuming and expensive legal procedures for your survivors, so if you really want to care for them and if you have any definite ideas about how you want your estate distributed, you must make a Spanish will. It's easy and you will feel more secure.

## Are You Bound By Spanish Law?

This Spanish law of obligatory heirs in theory applies to foreigners with property in Spain, restricting the disposal of this property just as it restricts such disposal for Spaniards. This is because most nations apply the law of the place where the property is located.

However, Article 9 of the Spanish Civil Code provides that, when a foreign property owner dies, even if he holds an official residence permit, the disposal of any assets he has in Spain will be governed by his own national law, not Spanish law. If his own country's law permits free disposal of the estate, this frees him from the Spanish law of "compulsory heirs" explained above. It does not free him from Spanish inheritance taxes.

This freedom applies only when such foreigner has an existing foreign will or Spanish will. If he dies intestate, without having made a will, Spanish law will be applied to his assets in Spain and they will be divided equally among his children.

This is a powerful argument for making a Spanish will disposing of your assets in Spain.

For citizens of the United Kingdom, the first complication arises here. A number of countries, including Great Britain, have laws stating that the disposition of real property such as land, houses and apartments will be governed by the law of the country where such property is located. English law — which applies to Wales and Northern Ireland in this case, but not to Scotland — also states that other assets, such as investments, will be governed by the law of the country where the deceased is legally domiciled at the time of his death.

So Spanish law says that English law will apply, and English law sends the ball right back, saying that *Spanish* law will apply, because that is where the property is located. An Englishman in theory is subject to the Spanish law, which may mean he can freely dispose of only one-third of his assets in Spain.

A number of other countries have laws similar to the English law. Investigate in your home country to find out what law applies to the disposition of real estate: the law of your home country or the law of the country where the immovable asset is located.

All this is the theory. Spanish law will apply to the disposition of foreigners' property located in Spain. It seems reasonable enough.

Wait a minute.

## Foreigners Have Free Disposition
### *But what happens in practice?*

In practice, any foreigner can make a Spanish will bequeathing his Spanish property to any person of his choice. He must declare that his own national law is ruled by the principle of free disposition of property by testament. The Spanish registrar of wills has so far accepted this, and when the time comes, the will is executed and the inheritor takes possession of his new property. Spanish lawyers routinely make such wills.

This means that, even if you are British, you can make a Spanish will leaving your Spanish property to whomever you choose.

The law also says that any foreigner officially resident in Spain is subject to Spanish inheritance law on his worldwide estate.

But in practice the authorities simply do not ask whether the testator is an official resident or not. They accept as valid the Spanish will disposing of only the Spanish property. The only requirement enforced by Spain is the payment of Spanish inheritance tax on property or assets located in Spain.

So most foreigners will find no problem in making a separate Spanish will to dispose of their immovable property in Spain, even though the law seems to say otherwise, whether they are residents or non-residents.

## Legitimate Inheritors Can Contest Spanish Will

*One note of warning.*

All of the above relating to the foreigner's making a will that permits him to leave his Spanish property to anyone he chooses, thus avoiding Spanish inheritance law which requires him to leave at least two-thirds of his estate to his children, works perfectly well in most cases. But, as we have said, it is not exactly in agreement with the law as written. It is more a matter of the Spanish authorities choosing not to enforce their own laws too strictly.

This means that, if you write your Spanish will leaving your lovely villa to your favourite daughter and cutting out your no-good son entirely, that son could get expert Spanish legal advice, contest the will on the grounds that the law stipulates that half of the inheritance is his, and win his case, thus getting title to half the villa.

So, if you foresee any possible challenge from one of Spain's legitimate inheritors, such as a child or a spouse, you should make other arrangements, such as transferring the title of the property to your chosen heir while you are still alive. You can always maintain the usufruct over the property, which gives you the right to use it as long as you are still living, although the title has formally passed to another person.

If you are quite certain that no possibility exists of successfully contesting it, then go ahead and make your Spanish will as you choose in the confidence that it will be executed as you have written it.

## Foreign Will Also

You also need to make a foreign will disposing of any assets you have in other countries. Be sure that any foreign will states clearly that it disposes only of your assets in that country and make sure to say in your Spanish will that it disposes only of your assets in Spain. There have been unfortunate cases where a person has made one will in Spain stating that all assets are left to one inheritor and another will later made in Germany or Australia, saying the same thing, but leaving "everything" to a different person.

In one particular case, the testator intended to leave all her German assets to family members and her Spanish villa to the friend who had looked after her for years. She made a Spanish will leaving everything to her friend in Spain and then made a German will, dated after the Spanish will, also leaving "everything" to her German family members. These inheritors later had the German will translated and legalized in Spain, and took possession of the Spanish property as well.

They were able to do this because the German will made no distinction of country and it was dated after the Spanish will, so it took precedence. So, the testator's wishes were not carried out and the faithful friend who had looked after the ill and dying person in Spain did not inherit the villa as she was supposed to.

This story is a good argument for taking legal advice when you make your Spanish will.

## Foreign Will Is Valid in Spain

Legally, it is not absolutely necessary for you to make a Spanish will to dispose of your assets in Spain. A :Briton who owns property in Spain can bequeath his Spanish apartment in the same British will he uses to dispose of his property in England, and his will can be executed in Spain. However, there are a number of steps which must take place in order to do this.

If you have lived in Spain for a long time it may be necessary for you to recreate a legal domicile in your home country for purposes of making a will. You may be able to do this by filing an official "letter of intent" with your lawyers. This letter states that, even though you hold a Spanish residence permit now, you really intend to return to your home country in the end. This should be sufficient for establishing a legal domicile in your home country and will allow its laws to apply.

Let us suppose that you are able to establish domicile in your home country and that its laws will apply. Your foreign will (which can be made at your Consulate in Spain as long as the proper formalities are observed) must go through the following process before it can dispose of your Spanish assets:

A certified copy of the grant of probate must be legalized by the Spanish Consul in the testator's home country, and a Spanish translation of this certified copy prepared. A Spanish lawyer must then be empowered to prepare a list of the assets in Spain, see that the Spanish inheritance taxes are paid, and handle the rest of the paperwork involved in distributing the assets.

Two lawyers registered in your home country, or a notary, or a Spanish Consul-General in your home country, must prepare a certificate of law, a *certificado de ley,* which affirms that the testator had the legal capacity to make a will; that the will is valid; that the Spanish law of obligatory heirs and the dispositions relating to property of spouses do not exist in the law of your country; that the will has been duly proved, and that the trustees named have the correct legal powers to administer the estate.

Finally, your will is declared effective to dispose of your assets in Spain, and your Spanish lawyer can carry this out.

It's a complicated, time-consuming and expensive process, and it is clearly better to make a Spanish will disposing of your assets in Spain.

## Making A Spanish Will

You go to see a Spanish lawyer and explain your wishes to him. In the case of the death of one spouse, for example, you may wish to leave all possible assets directly to the other spouse, without any inheritance to the children.

As a foreigner, you should be able to do this.

Even if surviving children inherit their legal portion, it is not usually necessary for the house to be sold and the proceeds divided, for example. The surviving spouse continues to live in the house and administer it for the good of the children still at home. If the house is later sold, the children can then get their legal share of the price.

The lawyer will advise you as to how the will should read in order to carry out your intentions. People sometimes say that they want their Spanish flat sold and the proceeds divided among the children, for example. Your lawyer will tell you that you cannot do this. You must leave the flat to the children in equal parts. They can then sell it and divide the proceeds, but you cannot order its sale in your will. There may be other provisions on which your lawyer can advise.

The will is made out in two columns, one in Spanish and one in English, or in whatever language the testator prefers. The will is then checked by the *notario* and signed in his presence and that of three witnesses. This is called a *testamento abierto,* an open will, which is the usual form. The notary keeps the original in his files, gives you an authorized copy and sends a notification to the central registry in Madrid, called the *Registro Central de Ultima Voluntad.* The certification numbers of all Spanish wills are kept on file here to ensure that a legal copy can always be found. If the will is lost or if you do not know whether the deceased person has made a Spanish will or not, you can apply to the central registry to find out if a Spanish will exists under that name. If it does exist, the registry will give you the number and the name of the notary who made it in the first place. You can get a copy of the will from the notary. Having a Spanish will certainly will speed up the legal processes of inheritance.

The notary will charge around 10,000 pesetas for the will and the lawyer's fee could be about the same, a total of 20,000 pesetas, although this could go much higher if the will is complicated or involves large sums of money.

Remember that husband and wife must each make separate wills, as they each own property separately.

## Inheritance Tax

You can also find out almost exactly how much inheritance tax your Spanish estate will attract. Your lawyer will consult the table of rates and then you will know what to expect. All too often, the existence of Spanish inheritance tax seems to come as a complete surprise to foreign property owners. This tax is charged even when the inheritance is between spouses, with only a minimum exemption, as explained in the next section.

## Secret Wills

Should you wish to keep secret the provisions of your will, you can also execute a *testamento cerrado,* a closed will. It is, of course, important to have a Spanish lawyer advise you to make sure your wishes square with Spanish law. Otherwise, you might find your desires cannot lawfully be carried out. You take this closed will, in an envelope, to the *notario,* who seals the envelope and signs it along with the witnesses. He then files it, just as with the open will.

Other types of wills are also valid.

You can make a holographic will, in your own handwriting, but this later has to be authenticated as genuine before a judge, which means more time, trouble and expense. You can even make a verbal will, in the presence of five witnesses. Each of the five witnesses then has to testify to the *notario* that these are truly the wishes of the deceased. The *notario* then prepares a written will and certifies it.

SECTION TWO

# Inheritance Tax in Spain

Spain's *Ley de Sucesiones,* which became law on January 1, 1988, makes inheritance tax lower than before, and many small inheritors will find that they pay no tax at all.

The present law provides a total exemption from taxes for inheritances under 2,655,000 pesetas.

The 2,655,000 exemption seems rather small, but it applies to each inheritor, not to the total estate. So, if you have a property worth 20 million pesetas, your half equals an estate valued at 10 million pesetas, and you leave it equally divided among your spouse and three children, each will receive an inheritance worth 2.5 million pesetas, and the bequest will attract no tax at all.

In addition, an inheritor under the age of 21 can have an exemption of up to 7,963,000 pesetas. For each year younger than 21, he deducts 664,000 pesetas more, until he arrives at the maximum at the age of 13.

This exemption applies to bequests between parents, children, spouses and brothers and sisters. For uncles, cousins and nephews, the exemption is cut by half to 1,330,000 pesetas. For more distant relatives, or those not related at all, there is no exemption.

The current law also reduces tax rates on bequests to uncles, nephews, cousins and non-relatives. Under the old law, an uncle or cousin receiving an estate of 10 million pesetas had to pay 48.72 per cent inheritance tax. The rate is now 18 per cent under the revised law.

Under the old law, if one were childless and wished to leave all his property to his best friend, the rate was extremely high. An estate valued at 10 million pesetas was taxed at 74.61 per cent. The present law provides for a rate of 22.95 per cent in this case, still quite high.

## Residents May Get 95% Free
### *Up to 20 Million Pesetas*

Since 1997, official residents of Spain leaving their Spanish property to wife or children may be eligible for a 95 per cent reduction in their tax base.

This reduction applies up to a maximum of 20 million pesetas. That is, if your inheritance is a property worth 20 million pesetas, you can reduce this total by 95 per cent, which comes to 19 million pesetas, and you pay tax on only one million pesetas.

But if your family home in Spain has a market value of 60 million pesetas, then half of that is 30 million. Your reduction stops at the maximum of 20 million, meaning you must pay Spanish inheritance tax on 10 million pesetas, which comes to just over one million pesetas in tax.

This reduction is also available for a principal dwelling left to a brother or sister over 65 years of age who has been living with the testator for the previous two years.

The reduction does not apply to any other property, such as a car or a yacht or shares in companies, only to the home itself.

The inheritor, in turn, must keep the property for at least 10 years. If she attempts to sell it, she will have to pay any tax due on the original inheritance.

This measure forms part of a package of laws designed to help small family businesses rather than retired foreigners. Many small business in Spain have failed on the death of the founder because his inheritors were unable to deal with the inheritance tax on the property, such as a shop or a small factory. Now the children can freely inherit, as long as they continue to operate the business for 10 years.

Retired foreign couples can also benefit, as described above, because the family home is included in the law. When one half of the couple dies, his or her share of the house or flat will be just about tax free to the surviving partner.

Non-residents cannot take advantage of this reduction.

## Rich Pay More

Those who are already rich will have to pay more in inheritance tax. The current law provides a sliding scale of tax rates by which a person who already has a large *patrimonio,* or net worth, must pay more. This rate can go as high as 85 per cent on an estate of more than 100 million pesetas left to a non-relative who already has a net worth of more than 600 million pesetas.

## How Does Spain Set Tax Values?

Spain has a set system for evaluating assets for purposes of inheritance tax. These are:

## REAL ESTATE

Property is valued either at market price, or at the *valor catastral,* or rated value, or at the value set by Hacienda for purposes of wealth tax, whichever is greater. So, in almost all cases, you will find that the declared sales price on your title deed, or today's market value, will be the value used. That is, if you bought your flat 20 years ago for 10 million pesetas, and it is worth 25 million on the market today, Spain's tax agency will value it at 25 million for purposes of calculating inheritance tax.

When you make your inheritance tax declaration, if you declare the flat as worth 20 million pesetas, you might get away with it, or you might get a notice from Hacienda that they have valued it at 25 million and you must pay tax on five million pesetas more.

Remember that Hacienda has its own office of valuation and is perfectly aware of the market price of real estate. They will not fine you, but they will charge you the extra tax. They do this frequently.

If you disagree with their valuation, you can request an independent survey, a *tasación*.

## PERSONAL EFFECTS

The furniture, clothing, personal possessions and so on of the deceased are called the *ajuar.* For inheritance tax purposes they are routinely valued at 3 per cent of the price of the property. If valuable works of art or antique furniture pieces are included, they may be valued separately. In general, add 3 per cent of the property value to your estate.

## AUTOMOBILES

Most property owners have automobiles, and these are included separately in the estate. Spain's Tax Agency publishes tables each year for the value of used cars. Other items, such as yachts or aeroplanes, will be valued separately.

## STOCKS AND SHARES

Stocks and shares in companies or mutual funds or other investments are valued at their price on the day of the person's death.

## LIFE INSURANCE

If received by children, the total amount is added to the estate, after a reduction of 1.5 million pesetas. If received by surviving spouse, half of the amount is added to the estate, and the other half is taxed as a capital gain in the spouse's yearly income tax. Spouse also has reduction of 1.5 million pesetas.

## BANK ACCOUNTS

The balance on the day of death is added to the estate.

Spanish Inheritance Tax Rates

### Year 2000

| Tax Base | Tax | Marginal Percentage |
|---|---|---|
| 0 | 0 | 7.65 |
| 1 330,000 | 101,745 | 8.50 |
| 2 659,000 | 214,710 | 9.35 |
| 3,988,000 | 338,972 | 10.20 |
| 5,317,000 | 474,530 | 11.05 |
| 6,646,000 | 621,384 | 11.90 |
| 7,975,000 | 779,535 | 12.75 |
| 9,304,000 | 948,983 | 13.60 |
| 10,633,000 | 1,129,727 | 14.45 |
| 11,962,000 | 1,321,767 | 15.30 |
| 13,291,000 | 1,525,104 | 16.15 |
| 19,926,000 | 2,596,657 | 18.70 |
| 26,561,000 | 3,837,402 | 21.25 |
| 39,831,000 | 6,657,277 | 25.50 |
| 66,351,000 | 13,419,877 | 29.75 |
| 132,702,000 | 33,159,299 | 34.00 |

### How to Use the Tax Table:
### *A Sample Calculation*

You can calculate your own inheritance tax by using the tables shown here.

First, figure your total value by referring to the section above on evaluations.

THE SPANISH PROPERTY GUIDE

## Reductions

You can then subtract from this amount any debts owed by the deceased. This would include a mortgage still unpaid on the property, for example. You can also deduct the expenses of the last illness and the funeral and burial.

## Refusal of Inheritance

In cases where the debts of an estate are greater than the assets, which could happen when a small business constitutes the estate, for example, the inheritors can refuse to accept the inheritance, thus being free of their parent's debts.

After you have made any deductions allowed you for the inheritance tax, such as your basic exemption of 2,655,000 pesetas if the estate is passing to close family, let's suppose that your final taxable inheritance is about seven million pesetas. Now you look at the table to find the nearest figure below that amount. In this case it is 6,646,000 pesetas and you have a tax due of 621,834 pesetas.

Now you need to consult the marginal percentage list, for the rate charged on the difference between the steps. In your case you find that you must pay 11.90 per cent of the difference between 6,646,000 and your seven million. The difference is 354,000 pesetas. Multiply this by 11.90 per cent and this gives you another 42,126 pesetas. Add the two together and you have a total tax of 663,960 pesetas, a little less than 10 per cent of your base.

These numbers were originally nice round numbers like three million or 10 million, but they have been increased according to inflation since the law was originally passed.

From this table, it looks as if 34 per cent is the absolute top rate of Spanish inheritance tax. This is true when the estate is passed in direct line of descent or between spouses. But it can be much higher when bequests are made to more distant relatives or to non-relatives. And it can be even higher when the inheritor is already wealthy. Remember that the sliding scale of Spanish inheritance tax is designed to favour the poor and soak the rich.

This scale provides multiplying coefficients for the degree of relationship and also for the amount of existing wealth of the inheritor. To get the amount of tax due from those who are more distant relatives or non-related and those who already have sizeable fortunes, you must multiply the basic tax rates above by the coefficients given in the table below.

| Existing Assets | Spouses Children | Cousins Uncles | Non-Relatives |
|---|---|---|---|
| 0 to 67 million | 1.0000 | 1.5882 | 2.0000 |
| 68 to 334 million | 1.0500 | 1.6676 | 2.1000 |
| 335 to 669 million | 1.1000 | 1.7471 | 2.2000 |
| More than 669 million | 1.2000 | 1.9059 | 2.4000 |

So, if you are fortunate enough to possess assets worth more than 669 million pesetas, and inherit more than 132 million pesetas from someone who is not related to you, the Spanish tax ministry will multiply the 34 per cent by the 2.4 coefficient and will demand a tax from you of 81.6 per cent.

This system penalizes inheritance to non-relations because it is designed to protect the family structure as well as the poor. It has caused problems for same-sex couples and for couples who may have lived together for many years in a stable relationship but are not married.

The high rate of inheritance tax and low exemptions in Spain cause many to seek ways round paying it, some of which are legal, some not.

## Can You Avoid Spanish Tax?

### Family Trust

Among the perfectly legal possibilities is the formation of a family corporation or trust, in which the family's wealth passes into the hands of the company, with each family member becoming a director of the company. So when one member of the family dies, it involves only a reorganization of the board of directors and a transfer of some of the company shares, attracting very little tax.

## Offshore Company

For non-Spaniards, the constitution of a Gibraltar-based company or other offshore operation in order to own real property in Spain has been another way to avoid Spanish inheritance taxes. In this case, when the founder of the company dies he leaves his shares to whomever he chooses in a will made outside of Spain. But as far as Spain is concerned, the same company continues to own the property and no transfer has taken place, hence there is no tax. See chapter on taxes for more information but be warned that Spain has placed a special tax on properties owned by companies registered in offshore tax havens. You will need expert legal advice on your individual circumstances and the possible disadvantages of this offshore ownership before you decide.

## Five-Year Limit

Another trick takes advantage of the fact that the statute of limitations on inheritance tax runs out after five years. That is, the State cannot collect the tax once five years have elapsed. So the scheme is to "lose" the deceased's will for five years, not declaring the property for inheritance. At the end of five years, the inheritor "discovers" the will and takes possession of the property, free of any inheritance tax. Where the estate is large and the tax is high, this plan can be worth it.

Be warned, however, that Spanish law requires that an inheritance be declared within six months of the death, and if you are found out, you can be subject to a surcharge of 25 per cent on the tax due, or even higher penalties if the Spanish authorities rule that deliberate fraud is involved.

Also be warned that the six-month period is included in the statute of limitations, so you really have to wait five years and six months.

You can also make a gift of the property to your inheritors while you are still living, perhaps reserving the right to inhabit the flat as long as you live, but remember that the Spanish gift tax is exactly the same as the inheritance tax.

## "Sell" Property Now

Or you might "sell" your property to your heir, again reserving the *usufructo* or lifetime right to inhabit it yourself. At property transfer costs of around 10 per cent, this could save your inheritor a sizeable sum when the valuation is more than 10 million and the inheritor is a non-relative.

You have to go on living for at least five years after you carry out this operation, however, or the State will assume that you did it only to avoid tax and will charge you the full amount.

This particular method has many attractions for same-sex couples where one party owns the property and wishes to leave it to the other, without suffering the very high rate of taxation applied to non-relatives.

Each case needs individual study so it makes sense to consult a Spanish lawyer when making your will.

## Summary

There are four points to bear in mind in connection with Spanish wills:

1.  You need to make a Spanish will disposing of your Spanish property in order to avoid time-consuming and expensive legal problems for your heirs. Make a separate will disposing of assets located outside of Spain.

2.  As a foreigner, you will probably find that Spanish authorities do not oblige you to follow the Spanish law of compulsory heirs, in which you must leave two-thirds of your estate to your children. You can leave your estate to whomever you choose, but you will be subject to Spanish inheritance tax, which can be high when property is left to non-relatives.

3.  There are very few ways around Spanish inheritance taxes and these legal ways require careful advance planning. Spanish law provides no large exemption from inheritance tax, such as most countries have when the family home is transferred. The tax is due after the first two and a half million pesetas.

THE SPANISH PROPERTY GUIDE

4.  However, if you are an official resident of Spain leaving your property to a spouse or child, you may be eligible for a 95 per cent reduction in the value of the property for inheritance tax calculation. This is not available to non-residents. Limit of 20 million pesetas.

184

## SECTION TWO

# Spanish Property Owners Community Handbook

## Comunidad de Propietarios

**A guide to your rights
and obligations in the
Community of Property Owners**

CHAPTER SEVEN

# Introduction

WHEN YOU BUY a property in Spain — as more than one million foreigners already have — you automatically become a member of a community of property owners, whether you like it or not. Whether the property is your retirement home or a holiday flat, whether it is an apartment, a townhouse or a detached villa on an urbanisation, you will find your own interests affected by the community and the decisions of your neighbours. You will pay your community fees every year, and you will meet with your neighbours at the Annual General Meeting to argue about whether to paint the outside of the building or whether to fire the gardener.

If your building or urbanisation is new, you may even take part in the original organisation of the community, with all its problems of drafting the statutes, electing a president, fixing the amount of community fees, planning the budget and defining the relation of the property promoter and his still unsold properties to the rest of the community.

Only those who buy an individual house in a town street or a farmhouse on a large tract of rural land will not have to deal with belonging to a Spanish *Comunidad de Propietarios*. A well-run community can add millions of pesetas of value to an otherwise unremarkable house, and a poorly-run community can cut millions off the value of even a very nice apartment.

Before you buy any Spanish property, find out as much as you can about the operations of the community. See the list of questions to ask in the Capsule Guide that follows.

Over the years problems arising from community life have produced hundreds of letters to my magazine column and many, many telephone calls to my radio programme. People want to know if the annual general meeting can be held in English, how to fire an administrator who is not properly serving the interests of all the owners, how to form a legal community on an unregistered urbanisation, how to collect community fees from non-payers, and hundreds of other matters.

This guide hopes to answer these questions.

Its aims are:

- *To help you understand your rights and obligations as a member of the community of property owners.*
- *To show you how to participate effectively in community life, both in and out of the Annual General Meeting.*
- *To make suggestions for dealing with problems that most frequently arise.*
- *To provide a ready reference to the complete English translation of Spain's Law of Horizontal Property, the law which regulates communities of property owners.*

Beware, however. If the law itself were perfectly clear to the normal citizen, we would not need lawyers to help us interpret it. This is just as true of Spanish law as it is of any other country's law.

So we have provided explanatory comments for each article of the law, telling how the rules work out in practice.

Keep in mind also that the English translation of the law is only informative. The real law is the one in Spanish.

Remember also that this book can only guide you in a general way. If there are serious disputes within your community which involve legal action, do not hesitate to obtain the services of a Spanish lawyer skilled in community matters. Often, a group of members can share the expenses. The courts of law are not an appropriate arena for the do-it-yourselves.

# Guide to Spanish Community Laws

## WHAT IS A COMMUNITY?

THE COMMUNITY OF PROPERTY owners - *comunidad de propietarios* - is the Spanish system for regulating the joint ownership of common property. In an apartment building this means the entrance way, the staircases, the lift, the roof space, the grounds and any other shared spaces used by all the owners. On an urbanisation it will include the roads, gardens, communal pools, lighting system, drains and other services.

This type of ownership is often called "condominium" in English, for co-ownership. The community sets out the manner in which all the co-owners manage their joint affairs for the best administration of the shared property. The co-owners must decide how much money they want to pay for the maintenance and management of their building, and how this money will be spent.

The law which regulates this system is called the Law of Horizontal Property - *la ley de propiedad horizontal*. This law, originally passed in 1960 and amended in April, 1999, is actually more vertical than horizontal because it applies mainly to apartment buildings, although it also covers townhouse developments of attached units.

Communities of owners on urbanisations of detached villas do not come under the Horizontal Law, although provisions of the new 1999 law make it easier for them to use the Horizontal Law's protection.

Urbanisations are regulated by other laws included in several sections of the Land Law, the *Ley del Suelo*. These communities may be of several sorts, but the most effective are called *entidad urbanistica colaboradora de gestión y conservación*. This mouthful translates as "collaborating urbanistic entity of management and maintenance," and is often shortened to EUC. Estates of detached villas require a different body of law because they present different problems. The roads, drains and lighting installations of the urbanisation may serve the public as well as the residents, thus having a quasi-public aspect which requires collaboration between the urbanisation owners and the Town Hall authorities. This interaction between the town and the estate demands extra regulation not needed in the case of apartment buildings.

But in both cases the idea of the law is the same: to provide a framework in which the community becomes a legal force. It can go to court, enforce the payment of community fees, make contracts. It can also be sued itself. Many problems have arisen in communities of detached villas because they were not originally formed according to the correct laws.

*SEE: Law of Horizontal Property, Articles 1 through 5, pp. 22-27.*

*Legal Communities for Urbanisations, p. 53.*

## Before you buy

When you buy property in Spain, you become a member of the community of property owners. You should know five things about this community before you sign any purchase contract.

## Ask these five questions:

## 1. How much will I have to pay each year in community charges?

Whether you buy an apartment, a townhouse or a detached villa, the property will have a participation share assigned to it, the *cuota*, which determines the amount of the yearly fees for community expenses. This can vary from as little as 5,000 pesetas a month in a modest apartment building up to 50,000 pesetas a month and even more on a luxurious urbanisation with many services to maintain.

These fees can be expected to rise with the general cost of living. The community members may have unexpected expenses, such as repairing the lift or the roof, or they may vote improvements which will add to the costs.

Keep in mind that community fees only cover the operating and maintenance of the building or estate. In addition, you will have to pay your individual annual real estate taxes and your water and electricity bills.

Ask your seller for his last paid-up community fee receipt. He is obligated by law to justify this or to declare the amount of the debt. If this is not possible, you can find out your property's share by asking the promoter of the building or the president of the community.

## 2. Are the community fees paid up to date?

The new Horizontal Law requires the President of the Community to produce a certificate stating that the property's fees are paid up, or listing the amount of the debt owed. The seller of the property should arrange for this. In any case, the buyer can be held liable only for the Community fees of this year and last year.

The law makes the seller responsible for unpaid community fees and for concealing any hidden debt which may attach to the property.

## 3. Can I see the community statutes?

Of course you can, and you can learn many things from them about life in your new property. Remember that the regulations of the statutes will be binding on you as a member of the community. If they prohibit dogs, you will not be able to keep Rover, for example.

Many sales contracts contain a clause in which the buyer states that he accepts the statutes of the community, understands them and agrees to abide by them. Even when there is not such a reference, the buyer is legally bound when he becomes the owner of the property. He cannot refuse to join a community which legally exists. (Some urbanisations do not, in fact, have a legal community).

Ask your seller, the president of the community, or the real estate promoter of a new building for a copy of the statutes. If they are not available, it may mean problems ahead for you, which brings us to the next question.

## 4. Does the community legally exist?

Sometimes a community of property owners does not have a proper legal existence, even when required by law. This can occur in a new building or urbanisation when sales are not yet completed and the community has not yet been constituted and its statutes registered with the Property Registry, in the case of apartment buildings, or the Registry of Conservation Entities, in the case of an urbanisation.

Yes, a properly constituted community is registered in the Property Registry. After all, it owns property, such as the garden spaces or the roads.

This legal vacuum can also occur when an established urbanisation either is illegal and unregistered or when the owners have formed their association under laws not properly designed for communities of property owners. Unless these associations of owners are registered and the new buyers agree in their contracts to abide by the statutes, their rules may not be legally enforceable.

Don't get too excited about disobeying the rules, by not paying the charges, for example, because Spanish courts have often ruled that such associations have a *de facto* existence, and a right to collect the fees for the common good.

Ask to see the legal registration of the community in one of the registries listed above.

If the community does not yet exist or is not properly registered, you will sooner or later have problems to sort out, either in the formation of the community or in making it a legal body. In either case, lawyers will be involved and there will be fees to pay.

## 5. Is the community in debt?

If the community has had to borrow money in order to pay for unexpected repairs on the building, you will assume your share of this debt when you become a member. Inform yourself in advance.

## See the Minutes Book

You can find out this and many other things by looking at the official minutes of the last Annual General Meeting of the community, along with the accounts.

Your seller should have a copy of the minutes and the accounts. If he has not, you can obtain them from the president of the community or from the promoter of the real estate where you are purchasing.

A reading of the minutes will give you an idea of the sort of problems and expenses that arise in this particular community. It will contain a record of the voting as well, so that you can see if one individual has voted the proxies of many others, as often happens in communities where many of the owners are absent from their properties much of the time.

If the minutes show that the principal business of the last meeting was how to deal with the persistent water problems or with the backlog of unpaid fees, you will know you have trouble ahead.

These official minutes will be in Spanish, but it will be well worth your time to have at least a rough translation made. The administrator or president of the community is obliged by law to keep these records at the disposal of the members.

*SEE: For proper registration of community, Law of Horizontal Property, Articles 5 and 6.*

*For community fees, see Article 9 .*

*For minutes of the meeting, see Law of horizontal Property, Article 19.*

## YOUR RIGHTS AND OBLIGATIONS

As a member of the community of property owners, you have the right to attend the annual general meeting, and any other meetings of the community, along with the right to be properly informed in advance of the dates and the order of business of any meeting called. If you are not correctly informed, you can protest and even have the results of the meeting annulled by a court.

At the meeting you have the right to voice your opinion, the right to vote, and to present motions for the vote of the other members.

You have the right to be elected and to hold office in the community. You may be the president, the vice-president or the secretary. You may be charged with administrating the affairs of the community.

You have the right to see all of the documentation and records of the community. The administrator or other officers are legally bound to keep these records and accounts at the disposal of the members. If they refuse to show them to you, you can obtain a court order to see the documents.

You have the right to hold and to vote proxies issued by other members who are absent from the meeting. This is common practice in communities where the foreign owners are absent much of the time.

Most communities in fact have a standard Proxy Form on which an absent member can delegate his vote to another member. If you win the confidence of many members and obtain enough proxy votes, you can run the community to suit yourself.

If you feel that a decision voted by the majority of the community is illegal or contrary to the statutes, you, acting alone, can ask the local court to rule on the matter. If you feel that the decision is legal, but seriously prejudicial to your own interests, and you can unite 25 per cent of the owners and shares, you can petition the court to have the decision annulled, or you can oblige the president to call an Extraordinary General Meeting. You will need skilled legal counsel for either of these actions.

You are obligated to pay the *cuotas* - community fees which have been properly voted by the members at the Annual General Meeting. If you do not pay, the community can claim the debt in court and even have your property sold at auction.

You are obligated to abide by the statutes of the community. If these statutes require all owners to paint their properties white and forbid owners to keep dogs, then you must paint your property white and you may not keep a dog. If you violate the statutes, the community members can vote to ask the court to issue an injunction which will forbid you from entering your property for a period of up to two years. This seldom occurs but the threat is there and it has been carried out in a few isolated cases.

Both the Law of Horizontal Property and the statutes of most communities make provision for such obligations as maintaining your property in good condition so that it does not cause damage to the other owners, and permitting workmen to enter your property when it is necessary for repairs on the building.

SEE: *Law of Horizontal Property, Articles 7 and 9.*

## THE PRESIDENT

The only community officer required by law is the president. He must be elected from among the members of the community, and he can carry out all the administrative work if no other officers are elected or appointed.

The president acts as the legal representative of the community in action. He signs contracts and cheques and can bring lawsuits in the name of the community when he is authorized by the vote of the general meeting. He himself can be sued by the community if the members feel his actions have prejudiced their interests. If the community is sued, perhaps by someone who fell through a badly-maintained balustrade, the president, acting through a lawyer, will be their representative in court. The president gives orders to the administrator.

The president will prepare the notices of general meetings, along with the order of business. He will see that the notices are sent out well in advance. He will oversee the preparation of the accounts of expenditures and income and he will prepare the budget for the coming year. He makes sure that the minutes of the meeting are carefully kept and notarized. He presides over the meeting and informs the absent members in writing of the decisions taken. If they do not register any protest within 30 days, their agreement to the decisions is assumed.

The president, when acting as the sole officer of the community, will oversee the management of the common elements of the property, will hear the complaints of the community members, and has full responsibility for the operation of the community, subject only to the approval of the annual general meeting.

The president is so important that the law says the community must never be without one. The usual term of office is one year, although the statutes may specify other time periods, but if the community does not act to elect a new president when the time is up, the old one continues in office until a new president is elected.

Many small communities where the president is the only officer find difficulty in persuading one of the members to take on this time-consuming responsibility. In many buildings, the flat owners take it in turn each year to be the president.

Under the new 1999 law, the president can even be paid for his services.

*SEE: For duties of the president, Law of Horizontal Property, Article 13.*

## THE ADMINISTRATOR

Because so many details demand the attention of the person who runs a community, most communities choose to name a professional administrator for this job.

The administrator is contracted to manage the services of the community and is paid a regular fee for this service.

Although many communities choose to employ a licenced *Adminstrador de Fincas,* or professional property administrator, or a licenced tax consultant or accountant, the community administrator need not hold any official title.

Many people think that the professional administrator is an elected officer of the community. This is not so. He is a hired professional, usually contracted for a period of one year.

The community may vote to renew his contract, vary his payment, or name a new administrator at the annual general meeting. The president may terminate the services of the administrator at any time if he feels that the administrator is not carrying out the duties specified in his contract. This decision must be submitted to the general meeting for approval, but this can take place after the action.

Relations between communities and their professional administrators have caused many problems. The administrator's contract must be very carefully drafted to make sure that both parties know their rights and duties.

The administrator's duties are the normal ones of seeing to the proper management of the common elements of the community. Unless otherwise specified in the statutes of a particular community, the horizontal law says that the administrator shall prepare the budget and present it to the meeting; maintain the building; inform the owners of his activities and carry out any other function conferred by the general meeting.

Many administrators carry out the work of the community effectively and rapidly, doing their best to keep all of the owners satisfied and well informed. They charge a reasonable fee for their services and they present the community members with clear accounts each year at the general meeting. These administrators are treasures.

In other cases, members complain that the administrators do not carry out the work for which they are responsible, that they arrange community affairs to suit themselves rather than the members, and that their accounts are vague and confusing, which leads the members to worry about where the money has gone. These administrators should be replaced.

Replacing the administrator, like electing the president, is an important step and will require the majority vote of the community members. This brings us to the Annual General Meeting, discussed below.

*SEE: For duties of the Administrator, Law of Horizontal Property, Article 20.*

## ANNUAL GENERAL MEETING

The Annual General Meeting is the maximum authority of the community of property owners, who are required by law to meet at least once each year to elect a president, discuss issues affecting the community, to examine and approve the accounts of expenditures of the previous year and to decide upon the budget - and the fees each member will pay - for the coming year.

The book of minutes, the *libro de actas,* which records details of the meeting and voting, is an official legal document which can be used in Spanish court proceedings. It must be stamped as authentic by a notary or a judge. This book establishes the right of the community president in court to bring a lawsuit against a community member who has not paid his fees, the *cuotas*. It records the names of members who voted in favour of a measure, either in person or by proxy, and the names of those who voted against each measure. This becomes important when a minority of community members wish to bring a legal protest against the decision of the majority, claiming that their interests have been seriously damaged, even though the majority vote was otherwise quite in order. In a court case, the dissenting minority must bring action against the majority. So the minutes book, as a legal document, establishes the names of those who voted on either side. The book is evidence in court, and decisions made by the community are serious matters.

Before you attend your first meeting, you should try to meet the president and the administrator of your community, as well as other members, to get an idea of the problems facing the members. If you already have a motion that you want passed by community vote, you can begin to assemble the proxy votes of members who support your position and who will be absent from the meeting. This proxy can be a simple written authorization that enables you to cast the vote of the absentee.

You must be notified at least eight days in advance of the meeting's date, time and place. You should also receive a written agenda, the order of business to be transacted, though this is not strictly necessary. The members can bring up any new business they wish at the meeting. It need not be listed on the agenda.

At the meeting, you will register your attendance, and any proxies you will vote, with the secretary or keeper of the minutes book.

The president will preside over the meeting. The first item will be the reading and voting to approve the minutes of the previous meeting. If the minutes do not meet with your approval, either because they are false or incomplete, you can vote against accepting them. Your protest will be registered in the book and can serve as evidence in court if you wish to make a claim.

The accounts of the previous year's income and expenditures will then be presented for the members' approval. You should have received your copy of these accounts before the meeting. Sometimes they are perfectly clear and other times they are quite incomprehensible. Ask the president, administrator or treasurer to explain any points not clear to you.

Then discussion will start on proposed plans and expenses for the coming year. Many issues can arise. Perhaps one group wishes to paint the building or to install a swimming pool, but others protest that this will raise the fees too high.

Tempers can run high at community meetings. They often degenerate into multilingual shouting matches when not properly managed. At one meeting a woman became enraged when she felt she was not getting her fair chance to speak and she threw an ashtray at the table of the presiding officers. A heavy ashtray.

Even in the best of circumstances, meetings tend to be long-winded, as different members insist on discussing minor details. One community I know voted unanimously to limit each member's speaking time to five minutes, and to limit each member to two speeches.

When it is time to vote, you will vote according to your *cuota*, or community share. This *cuota,* based on the size of your property, determines both your share of community fees and the weight of your vote. Usually, the majority of members is also the majority of the *cuotas*, but sometimes a few members with large properties can dominate the workings of a community. This can happen on an urbanisation where the developer still controls the votes of the unsold parcels of land and runs the community to suit himself.

The votes of the members will be recorded in the minutes book and action will be taken accordingly. A new president will be elected by majority vote and the building will be painted or not, according to the majority decision. There is always the possibility of protest, remember, when a minority of members feel they have been pushed around by the majority.

If a decision requires a unanimous vote, such as a change in the statutes or a construction project which will alter the participation shares of the community members, this unanimity can be achieved by informing any absent members of the decision. If they do not respond negatively within one month the motion is considered as passed unanimously.

One recent amendment to the horizontal law provides that the installation of ramps and other facilities for the handicapped requires only a three-fifths majority, even when such an alteration of the building would normally need a unanimous vote. This does not exactly give the handicapped a free rein, but it does improve their negotiating position. The new law came from a court case in which one person in a building had blocked the installation of ramps. This was perfectly legal although not very nice, and the Spanish Congress voted, in July 1990, to amend the law.

Finally the meeting will be adjourned, with some members pleased and others not pleased at all. This is truly democracy in action, with all its advantages and disadvantages.

When people are unhappy with their community, they always refer to it as "they." The community is never "they." It is always "we".

*SEE: For proxy votes, Law of Horizontal Property, Article 15 for annual general meeting, Article 14-18*

*For minutes book, see Article 19.*

# The Law of Horizontal Property in English

New Text of Law 49/1960 of July 21,
as amended by Law 8/1999 of April 6,
published in the Official State Bulletin April 8, 1999

## CHAPTER I:

## GENERAL DISPOSITIONS

### ARTICLE 1.

*The purpose of the present Law is the regulation of the special form of property ownership set out in Article 396 of the Civil Code, called horizontal property.*

*For the purposes of this Law, any part of a building which may be subject to independent use by virtue of an entrance either to the public thoroughfare or to a common area of the building itself shall be considered as "premises".*

### ARTICLE 2.

*This Law shall apply to:*

a) *Communities of Owners constituted under the provisions of Article 5.*

b) *Communities which meet the requirements established in Article 396 but which have not filed their charter or constitution as horizontal property.*

   *These communities shall be governed, in any case, by the dispositions of this Law in matters regarding the legal framework of ownership of the property, of its individual parts and of its common elements, as well as matters referring to the reciprocal rights and obligations of the community members.*

c) *Private real estate complexes (urbanisations or estates), in the terms established in this Law.*

## WHAT IT MEANS

The big news here for the new millennium is that urbanisations, or private housing estates, can be governed by the Horizontal Law, even if they have never registered their Statutes or constituted themselves legally as communities. If they meet the terms of Article 396 of the Civil Code, which basically means that the community shares some common elements, they can obtain the full force of the law in compelling the payment of debts and enforcing their rules.

Formerly, the only way for such non-registered urbanisations to obtain full legal status was through the complicated process of creating a Collaborating Urbanistic Entity. This still is necessary in some cases but the new provision of the 1999 law will permit many urbanisations to function as real communities.

## CHAPTER II:

*REGARDING THE SYSTEM OF OWNERSHIP BY FLATS OR BUSINESS PREMISES.*

## ARTICLE 3

*In the system of ownership set forth in Article 396 of the Civil Code, the owner of each flat or business premises shall have:*

a) *The unique and exclusive ownership rights over an adequately delimited area subject to independent usage, along with the architectural features and all types of installations, apparent or not, which may be included within its boundaries and which serve the owner exclusively, as well as any ancillary property expressly mentioned in the property deed, even when they are located outside the delimited area.*

b) *Co-ownership, with the other owners of flats and premises, of the remaining common areas, appurtenances and services.*

*To each flat or commercial premises there will be assigned a share of participation (cuota) relative to the total value of the property, expressed as a percentage of it. Said share (cuota) will serve as a basis to determine participation in the expenses and earnings of the community. The improvements or deterioration of each flat or premises will not alter the assigned share, which can only be changed by unanimous agreement.*

*Each owner may freely dispose of his property right, but he may not separate the elements composing it and any transmission of the property right shall not affect the obligations arising from this system of property ownership.*

## WHAT IT MEANS

The provisions of Article 3 are quite clear, setting out the terms of separate individual ownership of flats and the joint ownership of the common elements of the building. In paragraph A, the reference to "ancillary properties" means such things as garages or storage space in the basement which go with each apartment.

The final section of paragraph B establishes the principle that an owner may not subdivide his property. Later - in Article 8 - we shall see that he can indeed divide his property into smaller units, but this requires the consent of the community, as it will affect the participation shares.

## ARTICLE 4.

*The action of division shall not proceed to terminate the situation regulated by this Law. It can only be effected by each co-owner in regard to one flat or premises, is limited to that property, and providing that the joint ownership has not been established intentionally for the common service or use of all the owners.*

## WHAT IT MEANS

Article 4 makes it clear that any further action of subdivision of the property will not affect the scheme of Horizontal Property regulating the building in general. The last line means that a gardener, for example, who is given a flat in the building for his use, may not subdivide it. This action of division usually occurs when a property is inherited by several owners.

## ARTICLE 5.

*The charter of constitution of the condominium (ownership by flats or premises) will describe, besides the property as a whole, each one of those units to which a correlative number is assigned. The description of the overall property must express the details required by the mortgage legislation and the services and installations belonging to it. The description of each flat or premises will express its area, boundaries, the floor on which it is located, and any ancillary properties such as garage, attic or basement.*

*This same charter shall determine the share of participation that pertains to each flat or premises, to be set by the sole owner of the building at the beginning of its sale by flats, by the agreement of all existing owners, by arbitration, or by court order. For this determination, the useful surface area of each flat or premises relative to the total area of the building, its exterior or interior emplacement, its situation, and the use it can reasonably be assumed to make of the common services and installations shall be taken as a basis.*

*The charter may also contain regulations for the establishment and exercise of this property right and other dispositions not prohibited by law relating to the use and purpose of the building, its various flats or premises, installations and services, expenses, administration and management, insurance, maintenance and repairs, forming private statutes which shall not prejudice third parties if they have not been registered in the Registry of Property.*

*In any modification of the property title and apart from what is disposed regarding the validity of community decisions, the same requirements shall be applied as for the charter of constitution.*

### WHAT IT MEANS

In Article 5 we find several important points about the constitution of the community of owners. In the first paragraph the method of describing the property is set out. In the second paragraph, we find that each owner's *cuota*, or participation share, is fixed when the community is legally constituted and registered. Afterwards it can only be changed by unanimous vote of all members.

This paragraph also notes that the use each property makes of the common services shall be taken into account when setting the *cuotas*. This provision allows variation between flats and commercial premises, for example. Sometimes commercial premises pay a *cuota* per square metre higher than that of flats, on the grounds that the people they attract make extra use of common elements. In one case, the promoter of the building (who can set the *cuotas* when the flats are first sold) provided in the statutes of the community that the commercial premises would pay no *cuotas* at all until they were sold. This is because the flats always sell first and the commercial premises sometimes remain vacant for a year, or even more. By this means the promoter avoided paying any *cuotas* on his unsold business premises, and the community of owners had a lower income than they otherwise would expect.

This provision in the statutes - written by the promoter - is perfectly legal, even if unfair to the other new flat buyers, and is only one of the little tricks available to the promoter when he constitutes the community. It is always wise to read the statutes of the building or urbanisation where you are going to purchase.

In the case of the community cited above, the flat owners were preparing to vote against the promoter's rule in the statutes, charging that their interests were prejudiced by it.

Article 5 continues to note that the private statutes of the community will not be binding unless they are registered in the Registry of Property as part of the registration of the building itself.

It is perfectly possible for a community to exist without private statutes, which means that it will be regulated only by the terms set out here in the Horizontal Property Law. These regulations are sufficient for the orderly government of the community, but most buildings also require some special statutes to suit their individual circumstances.

THE SPANISH PROPERTY GUIDE

## *ARTICLE 6.*

*In order to regulate the details of their coexistence and the proper usage of the services and common elements and within the limits established by the Law and the statutes, the body of proprietors shall be able to make internal rules binding on all owners unless they are modified in the manner set forth for making decisions regarding administration.*

## WHAT IT MEANS

Article 6 is clear in itself. It allows the members of the community to make internal rules by majority vote. This would include matters such as the banning of pets or a requirement to make all awnings the same colour. This is the Horizontal Law for flats. In most urbanisations, such internal rules may only be enforceable when the new purchasers have specifically agreed to accept the statutes in their purchase contract.

However, as we shall see, the new 1999 law allows urbanisations to register their communities under the terms of the Horizontal Law, making their rules binding on the members.

## *ARTICLE 7.*

*The owner of each flat may modify the architectural features, installations and services of the flat, so long as it does not diminish or alter the safety of the building, its general structure, its form or its exterior condition nor prejudice the rights of another owner, reporting such alterations beforehand to the representative of the community.*

*In the rest of the building he shall not be able to make any alteration whatsoever and if he observes the need for any urgent repairs, he should communicate this to the administrator without delay.*

*The owner and the occupant of the flat are forbidden to carry on in the flat or in the rest of the building any activities which are not permitted in the statutes, are damaging to the property, are immoral, dangerous, unsuitable or unhealthy.*

## WHAT IT MEANS

Article 7 limits the owner's right to alter his property to interior elements only, and only when it does not threaten the structural soundness of the building or alter its appearance.

One problem that arises here is the closing-in of the terraces. Because the enclosure of the terrace with glass panels alters the exterior form of the building and would change the pattern of participation shares because of the greater enclosed area, it is strictly prohibited by this article.

So, when an owner goes to the community president and asks for permission to glass in his terrace, this must be denied. As you may notice, however, about 75 per cent of all the terraces in Spain have been glassed in. You guessed it. None of these owners asked anyone's permission. They just went ahead and did it.

If neither the community nor the Town Hall presents any complaint, the terrace remains enclosed. The possibility of protest does exist, however.

The final paragraph of this article lists activities forbidden to owners. Thus, dogs may be prohibited by the statutes, for example, and the owners must abide by this. If an owner ignores the statutory prohibition, the community, by majority vote, may take legal action against him. (See Article 19.)

## *ARTICLE 8.*

*Flats or commercial premises and their ancillary elements can be the object of physical division to form other, smaller independent units and made larger by the incorporation of adjoining units of the same building, or made smaller by the separation of some part.*

*In such cases, besides the consent of the affected property owners, there will be required the approval of the Annual General Meeting of the owners, to which pertains the determination of the new participation shares (cuotas) for the modified flats subject to the dispositions of Article 5, without altering the participation shares of the remaining properties.*

## WHAT IT MEANS

We saw in Article 3 that the right of an owner to divide his property in smaller units is limited, but it can be done. It requires, however, the approval of the Annual General Meeting.

## *ARTICLE 9.*

*The obligations of each owner shall be:*

a)  *To respect the general installations of the community and any other common elements, whether for general or private use by any of the owners, whether or not they are included in his unit, making appropriate use of them and avoiding any damage or deterioration at all times.*

b)  *To maintain his own flat and private installations in a good state of order in conditions that do not prejudice the community or the other owners, making good any damages caused by his lack of care or that of any persons for whom he is responsible.*

c)  *To permit in his flat or premises the repairs required for the service of the building and to permit in his flat the necessary rights of passage required for the creation of common services of general interest, voted according to the terms of Article 17, having the right to be indemnified by the community for any damage and prejudice.*

d)  *To allow entry into his flat for the purposes stated in the three preceding paragraphs.*

e)  *To contribute, according to the participation share (cuota) determined in his property title or according to any system especially established, to the general expenses for the proper upkeep of the building, its services, taxes, charges and responsibilities that are not subject to individual allocation.*

*Amounts due to the community deriving from the obligation to contribute to the payment of the general expenses which correspond to the fees assessed for the period up to date of the current year and for the previous year shall be deemed preferential debts under the terms of Article 1923 of the Civil Code and take preference for their settlement over those listed in paragraphs 3, 4, and 5 of that law without prejudicing the preference in favour of salary charges in the Workers' Law.*

*Any person acquiring a dwelling unit or commercial premises in the system of horizontal property, even with a title inscribed in the Property Registry, is held responsible, with the acquired property as guaranty, for the amounts owed by previous owners to the community for the payment of general expenses up to the limit of fees charged for the period to date of the year in which the purchase took place and for the immediately preceding year. The property itself is legally encumbered for the fulfilment of this obligation.*

*In the public contract or deed of sale by which the property is transferred in any way, the seller must declare that he is up to date with payment for general expenses of the community, or he must list what he owes. The seller must present certification of the state of his balance with the community, coinciding with this declaration, without which no public title can be authorised, unless the buyer should expressly waive the seller from this obligation. This certification shall be issued in a maximum of seven days from the request by the person acting as Secretary of the Community, with the authorisation of the President. In the case of fault or negligence, they shall be held liable for the accuracy of the information and for damages caused by delay in its issue.*

*f) To contribute, according to their respective participation shares (cuotas), to the reserve fund which shall exist in the community for the maintenance and repair of the property.*

*The reserve fund, which is held by the community to all effects, shall be supplied with an amount that in no case shall be less than five per cent of the last ordinary budget.*

*The community may use the reserve fund to take out an insurance policy covering damages to the property or to undertake a permanent maintenance contract for the building and its general installations.*

THE SPANISH PROPERTY GUIDE

g) *To observe due care in the use of the property and in their relations with the other owners and to be responsible to them for any infractions committed or damages caused.*

h) *To notify the person acting as Community Secretary, by any means which allows evidence of service, of their domicile in Spain for the purpose of receiving citations and notifications of any sort related to the Community. In the absence of this notification, the flat or premises in the Community shall be considered the domicile for receiving communications from the Community, and delivery to its occupant shall constitute full legal notification.*

*Should notification to the owner prove impossible at the place indicated in the previous paragraph, it shall be deemed to have taken place if the notice is posted on the notice board of the community, or in a visible place set aside for this purpose, indicating the date and the reasons for which this form of notification has been employed, signed by the person acting as Community Secretary and endorsed by the President. Notice served in this way shall produce full legal effect in three days.*

i) *To notify the person acting as Secretary of the Community, by any means providing certification of delivery, of any change in ownership of the unit.*

*Any owner who fails to comply with this obligation will be held liable to the Community jointly with the new owner for debts incurred after the transfer, without prejudicing his right to claim repayment from the new owner.*

*These terms shall not apply when any of the governing bodies of the community established in Article 13 have been notified of the change of owners by any other means or by definite actions of the new owner or when the transfer is publicly known.*

*2. For the application of the preceding regulations, expenses will be deemed as general when they are not imputable to one or several flats, nor shall the non-usage of a service bring exemption from the fulfilment of the corresponding obligations., subject to the terms of Article 11.2 of this Law.*

## WHAT IT MEANS

The first paragraphs of this Article set out owners' obligations clearly enough.

Paragraph E tells us that the new buyer in a community is held responsible only for the community fees of this year and the year before, with the property itself acting as the final guarantee for payment.

This paragraph also tells us that the seller is obliged to present certification of payment up to date or the amount of his debt at the time of signing the contract, which means at the Spanish notary's office. The President of the Community must vouch for this certification.

Further, without the certification of payment or debt, the Notary will not stamp the contract of sale, unless the buyer specifically waives the requirement.

Paragraph F provides for the establishment of a reserve fund in all communities, which must be at least five per cent of the normal operating budget, and sets out the obligation of each owner to contribute to this fund. The fund can be used for an insurance policy or a maintenance contract, thus protecting the installations.

Paragraph H requires every member to notify the Community of the address in Spain where he wishes to receive any legal notices. One way to do this is to use the Burofax system of the Spanish postal service. They will certify both the content of the message and its delivery. Lacking an address, the Community can notify the owner at the property itself, and, if for some reason this cannot be done, simply posting the notice on the notice board will take full legal effect within three days.

This is a big change from previous practice, which made the notification so complicated that Communities just gave up trying.

This procedure used to be so difficult and time-consuming that it was hardly worthwhile in most cases. The community had to prove that the defaulter had received in a certified manner each of the unpaid bills, and that he had been informed of the debt and had acknowledged receipt, and every stage of the process was complex.

The last paragraph of this article settles another common dispute. Sometimes an owner will declare that, because he does not use the swimming pool, which he voted against in the meeting, he will not pay this portion of his community charges. This line says he is obliged to pay, abiding by the majority decision.

Even so, in many communities, the members will vote to exempt non-users from the payment for a particular amenity.

### ARTICLE 10.

*1. The Community is obligated to carry out work necessary for the proper upkeep and maintenance of the building and its services to ensure adequate structural, waterproof, habitability and safety conditions.*

*2. Any owners who unjustifiably oppose or delay the execution of orders issued by public authorities shall be held responsible individually for any administrative fines that are charged as a result.*

*3. Disagreements concerning the nature of works to be carried out shall be resolved by the General Assembly of Owners. The parties may also apply for arbitration or for a technical report in the terms established by law.*

*4. The payment of expenses arising from maintenance work referred to in this article shall attach to the flat or premises in the same terms and conditions set out in Article 9 for general expenses.*

### ARTICLE 11.

*1. No owner can demand new installations, services or improvements not required for the adequate maintenance and habitation of the building, in accordance with its nature and characteristics.*

*2. When decisions are lawfully made to carry out improvements not required in accordance with the terms of the preceding paragraph and the proportionate cost of installation exceeds the amount of three ordinary monthly payments for common expenses, a dissenter shall not be obligated, nor shall his fee be altered, even in the case that he cannot be deprived of the improvement or innovation.*

*If the dissenter wishes at any time to take advantage of the improvement he must pay his share of the expenses of installation and maintenance, brought up to date by application of the legal interest rate.*

*3. Innovations which render any part of the building unserviceable for the use and enjoyment of an individual owner shall require his express consent.*

*4. Special assessments for improvements made or to be made in the community shall be charged to the owner of the property at the time when such payments fall due.*

## WHAT IT MEANS

Article 11 requires some careful interpretation and amplification. There is more in it than it seems to say.

The first paragraph seems clear enough. No single owner or minority group can demand unnecessary improvements. The definition of "necessary" is here related to the building's category or standard of luxury. Central air-conditioning may be "necessary" in a luxury building. A swimming pool or satellite TV will not be necessary in a modest block of flats, and no single owner can demand it.

Majority rules.

It's what this paragraph doesn't say that is more important. It implies that one single owner can demand "necessary" improvements, with legal right on his side. That is, there exists in law a principle that the property must be properly maintained.

If the majority of owners refuses to repair the broken lift, fix the broken windows or doors, one single owner can demand of the court that the community be obliged to carry out this normal maintenance. He can cite this article, along with Article 16, to back up his case.

217

He will find additional support if the building has become a health or safety hazard, as the community's decision to let it fall into ruin will then run contrary to law.

Of course, honest dispute is also possible about what constitutes "necessary" and people can spend hours arguing this in the community meeting.

In the second paragraph of Article 11, we find another sore point relating to "necessary" improvements. If the Annual General Meeting votes to carry out some improvement which is clearly not required for adequate maintenance, and the cost of this improvement exceeds the amount of three months community *cuotas*, a dissenter can legally refuse to pay for it. This could be a new swimming pool, for example.

Even though the next two lines make reference to his eventual payment should he wish to make use of the improvement, Spanish courts have ruled that the dissenter cannot be deprived of the use of the improvement even though he does not pay for it.

Paragraph 3 gives the individual owner the power to block any change in the building which would affect his use and enjoyment of the property. This would include the building of a wall in front of his window, for example.

Paragraph 4 settles an area where confusion may arise.

The new owner of the property might refuse to make the next payment on a new swimming pool which was voted before he bought his flat. He can't do that. He assumes all the Community expenses and projects when he becomes a member.

The same principle applies if the Community has previously voted to make special assessments in order to pay off a debt which existed before our new buyer came in. He must pay his share as he is the owner when the payment comes due.

He cannot charge the debt to the previous owner, even if the debt was incurred in the previous owner's time and has nothing to do with the new owner.

## ARTICLE 12.

*The construction of new floors and any other change in the supporting structure or walls of the building or in the common elements affect the charter of constitution and must be submitted to the procedures established for modifications of it. The resolution which is adopted shall determine the nature of the modification, the alterations it produces in the description of the property and the flats or premises, the variation of the participation shares (cuotas) and the owner or owners of the new premises or flats.*

## WHAT IT MEANS

Article 12 is clear enough. When it says that any major modification of the structure must be submitted to the same procedure as for changes in the community's charter, it means by unanimous vote. The resolution so passed must be specific and completely detailed.

## ARTICLE 13.

*1. The governing bodies of the community shall be the following:*

*a) The General Assembly of owners.*

*b) The President and, when applicable, the Vice-Presidents*

*c) The Secretary*

*d) The Administrator*

*The Statutes or a majority vote by the General Assembly may establish other governing bodies for the Community but these may not detract from the functions and responsibilities with regard to third parties which this Law confers on those mentioned above.*

*2. The President shall be chosen from among the owners in the Community by election or by turns in rotation or by drawing lots. Acceptance shall be compulsory, although the designated owner may request the Court to relieve him of the office, within one month of taking office, citing his reasons for it. The Court, following the procedure established in Article 17.3, will rule on the matter, designating in the same ruling which of the owners will substitute for the*

*President in the office, until a new President is chosen in a time set by the Judge.*

*Likewise, the Court may be approached when it has proved impossible for the Assembly to choose a President for some reason.*

*3. The President legally represents the Community both in and out of court and in all matters affecting it.*

*4. The existence of Vice-Presidents is voluntary. They shall be chosen by the same procedure established for the designation of the President.*

*The Vice-President or Vice-Presidents in the order prescribed, shall replace the President in cases of absence, vacancy or incapacity and assist him in carrying out his duties according to the terms established by the General Assembly.*

*5. The functions of secretary and administrator shall be carried out by the President of the Community, except when the Statutes or the General Assembly, by majority vote, provide that such office be held separately from the presidency.*

*6. The posts of Secretary and Administrator may be vested in the same person or separately chosen.*

*The posts of administrator or secretary-administrator may be held by any owner or by individuals with sufficient professional qualifications or legally licenced to carry out such functions. The post can also go to a company or other corporate entity in the terms set out by law.*

*7. Unless otherwise provided by Community Statutes, the term of office of all governing bodies will be for one year.*

*The persons designated to can be removed from their offices before the expiry of their terms by a resolution of the General Assembly, convoked for an extraordinary meeting.*

*8. When the number of owners in the community is no more than four, they can govern themselves by the administrative system of Article 398 of the Civil Code, if their Statutes expressly establish this.*

## WHAT IT MEANS

Article 13 states that the president must be a member of the community. A simple majority vote in the Annual General Meeting suffices to elect him, and a simple majority vote can put him out, along with any other officer of the community.

There is nothing in the rule book that says the president must speak Spanish, or be Spanish, or even an official full-time resident of Spain. It would be difficult for an absentee president to serve his community well, of course, but the only requirement is that the president be a member of the community.

By law, the president is the only officer that a community must elect. He can combine in himself the duties of the secretary, treasurer and administrator, and in many smaller communities this is the case. In larger blocks - sometimes numbering more than 100 members - communities may elect a vice-president to stand in for the president when he is absent, a secretary to keep the official minutes book of the meetings, a treasurer to take charge of the funds, and appoint a professional administrator to handle the maintenance of the property. The professional administrator, paid for his services, may not in principle be a member of the community as this would be an obvious conflict of interests.

The community can see that the President's expenses are covered and they can even pay him a wage if they choose.

The responsibilities of the president include:

Convening the Annual General Meeting, giving reasonable advance notice, along with the order of business. Any owner who was not properly notified of the meeting can later protest and have the results of the meeting annulled by a judge.

Presiding over the general meeting, seeing that the order of business is followed and making sure that each person gets a fair hearing. This can be a very arduous task.

Representing the community in its relations with the individual members. That is, if you have a complaint about water dripping from the terrace of your upstairs neighbour, you take this complaint to the president.

Representing the community to all third parties, which would include the company contracted to paint the building. It is the president who signs the contract in the name of the community.

Carrying out any legal action for which he has been authorized by the majority vote of the owners assembled in the general meeting.

It is a serious matter to be president of a legally-registered community of property owners. The president cannot simply resign his office, for example, if things do not go well. He officially holds the post until a new president is elected. This is because the community can never be without a legal representative. So, if the president wants out, he must convene an extraordinary general meeting for the election of his successor or petition the Court to relieve him.

Further, if the community members feel that the president, through negligence or error, has seriously damaged their interests, they can bring suit against him for monetary damages.

Normally the president is elected for one year, unless the community statutes specify a longer term of office. At the end of this year, his mandate will continue unless the general meeting votes to replace him. So it is perfectly possible for a president to continue in office year after year without any new elections.

If any member of the community wants to contest this continuance, he can either ask for an election notice to be included in the agenda of the meeting, or he can call for elections in the meeting itself. Remember that the Annual General Meeting is the supreme authority of the community. It can, by majority vote, elect a new president whenever it desires to do so. The normal procedure would be to convoke an extraordinary general meeting for this purpose. Remember also, that whenever 25 per cent of the members agree, they can call for such an extraordinary general meeting.

This unpaid job of president is often so unrewarding that, in some buildings, rather than actually hold elections, the community members agree to take the post in turns, with a different member taking up the task each year. When your turn comes, you are unanimously "elected" and this is shown in the Minutes Book.

If the community chooses to contract a paid professional administrator, the president can hire and fire this adminis-trator, subject always to the specific contract made, giving account later to the community.

Sometimes community presidents act in a high-handed manner, spending the funds incorrectly and favouring one group of owners over another. This might happen when one member controls many votes. Far more often the presi-dent is a civic-minded spirit who is willing to take his turn at handling the problems which arise in any community, only to discover that his co-owners find fault with every decision he makes and are utterly ungrateful for his efforts to help the common good. So he is vastly relieved when his term of office ends and he absolutely refuses to be elected again.

If the community chooses to name a secretary, his func-tion will be the normal work of a secretary in any organiza-tion: to send or deliver the notices of meetings; to take the minutes of the meeting and see that they are recorded in the official *libro de actas* , or minutes book, which is stamped by the Notary; to keep the records, correspondence and docu-ments of the community and to show these to any member who wishes to inspect them, and to send out notification of the decisions taken in the annual general meeting to any absent members. This is obligatory. Members who were absent from any meeting must be reliably informed of any decisions taken at that meeting. They then have 30 days starting from the date they received the notification, in which to make a protest if they are opposed to the decision. If they do not make a written protest, they are considered as accepting any action taken by the meeting. If the meet-ing has adopted a measure needed unanimous approval, the non-reply of the absentees is included as approval, thus making the vote "unanimous".

Although the law of horizontal property does not require a vice-president or a treasurer, the community statutes can provide for the election of these officers, or the members may vote at the annual general meeting to create the offices and elect members to carry them out.

The treasurer would prepare the proposed budget of expenses for the forthcoming year for the approval of the meeting; would collect and keep the funds of the community; would be responsible for the accounts, and make payments and prepare the yearly accounting for the members' approval. He might also order an independent auditing of the accounts, specially if the community is a large one with important sums of money coming in and going out.

An important point to note about a possible vice-president in a community is that this office must be specifically mentioned, with its powers, in the statutes or in the official minutes book of the community. If not, the vice-president will not be empowered to use the faculties of the president in his absence. He will not be able to sign cheques, represent the community or take legal action.

Article 13 closes with a mention of Article 398 of the Civil Code, which provides a much simpler legal framework for organizing the affairs of communities with four or fewer members.

### *ARTICLE 14.*

*The functions of the Annual General Meeting are:*

a) *To appoint and to remove the persons who hold the official posts mentioned in the preceding article and to settle any complaints which the property owners may bring against their actions.*

b) *To approve the budget of foreseeable expenses and income and the pertinent accounts.*

c) *To approve bids and the carrying out of all repair work on the property, whether ordinary or extraordinary, and to be informed of any urgent measures taken by the Administrator in accordance with the terms of Article 20, paragraph c.*

d) *To approve or change the statutes and to make bylaws for internal management.*

e) *To be informed and to decide on the other matters of general interest to the community, taking any necessary or advisable measures for the best common service.*

## WHAT IT MEANS

Article 14 states the basic functions of the Annual General Meeting. The general meeting, ordinary or extraordinary, is the supreme authority of the community. Its decisions, either by majority vote or unanimous vote when necessary, are binding on all officers and members of the community.

Majority vote will elect the officers and also put them out if necessary. If the members are unhappy with the president, for example, they themselves can convoke an extraordinary general meeting, and vote him out. If they have contracted a professional administrator for one year, they can vote at the meeting not to renew his contract.

The meeting will hear the budget of expenses prepared for the coming year. They must approve the expenses or the officials will not be empowered to spend the money. It is here that the fighting often starts. Does the community need a full-time gardener? Should they paint the building or let it go another year? Each point of view will have its backers. They present their opposing arguments, a vote is called, and majority rules. If a dissenter feels his own private interests are seriously damaged by a decision of the majority, he has the power to protest before a court.

The community must also approve the accounts presented for the preceding year. Here again there are often many protests, as some presidents and even some professional administrators often fail to keep adequate records. This is sometimes due to concealment of payments to the administrator but more often results from careless bookkeeping. Many larger communities are beginning to require an independent audit of the accounts as a regular yearly practice.

The third item of the functions of the annual general meeting is probably the one that causes most fireworks: the execution of extraordinary works and the necessary funding. In every community there is someone who wants a swimming pool, or a new lighting system, or satellite television. And in every community there is someone who does not want these things and says he will refuse to pay for them.

Remember that a dissenter can refuse to pay - legally - if the improvement is not 'necessary" and if his share of it comes to more than three month's *cuota*.

The annual general meeting has the power to change the statutes - but only by unanimous vote - and to make internal regulations. These would include things like the prohibition of pets in the building, for example, or the denial of permission to hang out laundry on the roof terrace.

Of course the members must have information in order to decide matters of general interest to the community, as noted in the final section. This means that the administrator and president must present complete information to the meeting. It is their legal obligation to allow community members to examine the community's accounts and documents.

Paragraph C makes special mention of the Assembly's right to be informed by the Administrator of any urgent measures he has taken. Administrators sometimes treat communities as their own property and fail to keep the members well informed of their actions.

## *ARTICLE 15.*

*1. Attendance at the general meeting of owners shall be in person or by legal or voluntary representation, a written authorization signed by the owner being sufficient to accredit this representation.*

*If a flat belongs jointly to several owners, these shall name one representative to attend and to vote in the meetings.*

*If the flat is held in usufruct, the attendance and the
vote belong to the original owner who, except for his mani-
festation to the contrary, shall be held to be represented by
the holder of the usufruct, this representation requiring to
be specifically expressed when the vote is on the matters referred to in the First paragraph of Article 17 or on extraordinary works or improvements.*

*2. Owners who at the time of the Assembly are not cur-
rent in the payment of all their debts owed to the Community, and who have not legally challenged these debts or deposited the amount of them in court shall be allowed to take
part in discussion but shall not have the right to vote. The
minutes of the meeting will show the names of the owners
deprived of their voting rights and neither the person nor
the participation share shall be computed when calculating
the majorities required by this Law.*

## WHAT IT MEANS

The first paragraph of Article 15 makes provision for the
representation of a community member by proxy if he cannot attend in person.

A simple "written authorization" is sufficient to establish this proxy legally. There is no specific form required.
All it need say is that you authorize such-and-such a person to vote in your name at the meeting of the community
on such-and-such a day, and it should include the phrase,
"any postponement of that meeting," because very often the
community does not have a full quorum when the meeting
is first called and so it will be held on the 'second convocation," usually specified as half an hour later.

But this sort of open proxy can be dangerous if you do
not fully trust the person exercising it. He can vote against
your best interests if he chooses. You can also make a specific and detailed proxy, which authorizes its holder to cast
your vote only in certain ways. That is, the proxy can declare that its holder must vote "yes" on items three and five
of the meeting agenda and can vote "no" on items one and
four, and that he must abstain from voting on the other

issues. The secretary of the meeting will ask to see the proxy forms when he registers each member's attendance at the meeting, so he will know this.

Most communities have proxy forms already printed and available from the secretary, but they are the open sort, so you must make your own if you want to be specific. There is no provision for absentee voting by post.

Proxies have caused many problems in communities. Foreign owners absent from Spain tend to give their proxy to some influential person in the community. This person is often the developer of the building, who still has unsold units, and so is a member of the community. He votes the shares of the unsold flats still in his name, along with the proxies he has been given, and can often control the operations of the community in this way. Or it may be the president who keeps himself in office with these proxies. In one case, it was the representative of a rental agency which owned some flats in a building and managed others. With the proxies the agency controlled, they ran the building to suit the renters and to the disadvantage of the permanent residents. So there are many tricks available with proxies.

Article 15 also refers to flats held in usufruct. This means that the owner has granted the right to occupy the flat to another person, as sometimes happens when the property is held in the name of a son or daughter. The son or daughter, by a legal document, grants to the parent the lifetime right - usufruct - to inhabit the property. This is sometimes done in order to skip over one generation of inheritance taxes. When the parent dies, the son or daughter simply takes possession of the property which has always been his. The holder of this usufruct is considered the owner's representative at the community meeting for all normal matters. If, however, the community is voting to change its statutes or to authorize extraordinary works, then the holder of the usufruct will need a specific written authorization from the owner of record.

Paragraph 2 of the article contains the real change in the new law. For the first time, community debtors are both deprived of the right to vote and are listed for all to see. Unless these debtors have impugned the court decision against them and deposited the funds, they cannot vote.

## ARTICLE 16.

*The general meeting of proprietors will be held at least once a year to approve the budgets and accounts and at any other time the president considers it advisable or when one quarter of the owners request it, or any number of owners who represent at least 25 per cent of the participation shares.*

*The president shall convoke the meeting and, in the absence of this, the promoters of the meeting, giving notice of the agenda of business, the time, day and place of the meeting for the first call, and, when applicable, the second call. Notification shall be given in the form set out in Article 9. The notice of meeting shall contain a list of the owners who are not current in the payment of debts to the Community and will warn of the loss of the right to vote under the conditions expressed in Article 15.2*

*Any owner can request the General Meeting to examine and resolve on any matter of interest to the Community.*

*For this purpose he should present to the President in writing the clearly specified points he wishes dealt with. The President shall include them in the agenda of the following General Meeting.*

*If the majority of owners, representing at the same time the majority of participation shares (cuotas) are not present at the time of the first call, the meeting shall be convened again on second call, without the need for a quorum.*

*The meeting shall be held on the second call at the time, date and place indicated in the first notification. It can be held on the same day, as long as at least half an hour has passed since the first call.*

*Failing this, it shall be convened again, according to the forms established in this Article, within eight days following the meeting not held. In such case, notification must be made at least three days before the meeting.*

*3. Notification of the ordinary Annual General Meeting
will be given at least six days beforehand and, for extraordinary meetings with as much advance notice as possible so
that it can come to the attention of all the parties involved.
The general meeting can lawfully take place even without
the convocation of the president, providing that all of the
proprietors agree and decide this.*

## WHAT IT MEANS

Article 15 states that, by law, a general meeting must be
held at least once a year. The only item of business legally
required is the approval by the members of the accounts
and budget. It is not strictly necessary to hold elections for
a new president because the old one will continue in office
until he is replaced by majority vote.

But the expenses must be approved by a legally-registered vote of the community members. It is perfectly possible for them to decide that they will not pay out any money
for the next year. This means, of course, that the electric
company will cut off the lights and the building's insurance
policy will lapse. But no money can be spent without the
majority vote of the members.

This annual general meeting is the ordinary meeting.
Other meetings, known as extraordinary meetings, may also
take place. The president may call such a meeting at any
time, giving adequate notice.

This question of what constitutes "adequate" notification is a little tricky, especially when three quarters of the
members of the community are residing in another country
at any particular moment, but any president will try to give
sufficient notice because he knows that a member who feels
he has not been correctly warned of the meeting can protest
and a court may rule the results of the meeting void.

An extraordinary meeting can also be called whenever
one quarter of the members of the community, or people
who represent one-quarter of the participation shares, request it. The president is then obligated to convene the
meeting.

In the case of the president's absence or incapacitation, the promoters of the meeting may also convoke it.

The law mentions one-quarter of the participation shares, or *cuotas*, because in many cases one or two owners may control a much larger share of the building than the owner of a single flat. One such example would be a large department store that holds more than one-quarter of the *cuotas* all on its own. Another would be the developer himself, who controls and votes all the shares of the unsold flats. This situation, in which one owner holds great voting power, has caused problems in more than one community.

It is common practice for the second calling of the meeting to appear on the original notification, usually set for a half hour after the first calling.

This means that, if a majority of members or cuotas is not present — and often it isn't — the meeting can still take place, no matter how few owners or shares are present. Their decisions will be perfectly valid if not protested by the other owners within 30 days after they are notified of the actions.

## ARTICLE 17.

*Decisions of the general meeting shall be subject to the following rules:*

*1. Unanimity shall only be required for the validity of those resolutions which involve approval or modification of rules contained in the charter of constitution of the property or in the Community Statutes.*

*The establishment or elimination of the lift, janitor, reception desk, security services or other common services of general interest, even when they involve modification of the charter of constitution or the Community Statutes, shall require the vote in favour of three fifths of the total number of owners, who at the same time represent three fifths of the cuotas, or participation shares. The leasing out of common elements which have no specific use assigned them in the building shall also require the favourable vote of three fifths of the total number of owners who, at the same time represent three fifths of the participation shares, as well as the consent of the owner directly affected, should there be one.*

*Work executed or new common services established to eliminate structural barriers which hinder the access or mobility of handicapped persons, even when this involves the modification of the charter of constitution or the Community Statutes, shall require the favourable vote of a simple majority of the owners, who at the same time represent the majority of the cuotas.*

*For effects established in the preceding paragraph, the votes of correctly notified owners absent from the meeting shall be computed as favourable when, having been informed of the decision taken by those present, in accordance with the procedure set out in Article 9, they did not express dissent to the person acting as Community Secretary within 30 days, by any certified means of delivery.*

*Decisions validly taken according to the dispositions of this rule are binding on all owners.*

*2. The installation of common facilities providing access to telecommunication services regulated in Royal Decree-Law 1/1998 of February 27, or the adaptation of existing systems, as well as the installation of solar energy systems, whether common or private, and facilities necessary for obtaining new collective energy sources, may be agreed, at the request of any one owner, by one third of the members of the community representing one third of the cuotas.*

*The Community shall not charge the cost of the installation or adaptation of the above-mentioned facilities, nor the costs arising from its conservation and maintenance, to those owners who did not expressly vote in the meeting in favour of the decision. Nevertheless, if they later request access to the telecommunication system or to the energy supplies and this requires the use of the new facilities or the adaptations carried out on the preexisting systems, this can be granted, providing that they pay the amount which would have corresponded to them, correctly brought up to date by applying the corresponding legal interest.*

*Without prejudice to the above-mentioned expenses of up-keep and maintenance, the new facilities shall have the status, to all effects established by this Law, of common elements.*

*3. For the validity of all other resolutions, the favourable vote of the majority of the owners which at the same time represents the majority of the cuotas shall suffice.*

*On the second calling of the meeting decisions voted by the majority of those present, provided that they represent more than half the participation shares present, shall be valid.*

*When a majority cannot be achieved by the procedures established in the foregoing paragraphs, the Court, at the petition of one of the parties within a month of the date of the second meeting, and hearing any dissenters, who must be duly notified, will rule in equity within 20 days of the petition, and will rule on the assignment of legal costs as well.*

## WHAT IT MEANS

Under the previous Law of Horizontal Property, a unanimous vote was required for any modification of the building, which led to necessary and useful action being blocked by one or two dissenters.

The new law sets out very carefully the sort of actions which now require only a three-fifths majority.

It also notes that your vote will be counted as favourable if you were absent from the meeting and did not protest within 30 days of being informed, and you will then be bound by the decision of those present at the meeting.

Sometimes a very small number of owners really make the decisions for the Community.

If you are baffled by references in this Article to access to telecommunications, don't worry. They mean communal television aerials, which require only a one-third vote in order to bind all of the owners. The same goes for work to install any renewable energy source.

All other Community votes require only a simple majority, including the election of the President.

And if you are puzzled by the requirement that this majority must be a majority of the number of owners present as well as a majority of the amounts of participation shares, or cuotas, this is understandable.

When there is a conflict; when, for example, one owner controls many shares because he owns ten apartments in the building or for some other reason, Spanish courts have usually ruled in favour of the number of owners rather than the amount of cuotas when deciding a contested vote.

## *ARTICLE 18.*

*1. Decisions voted by the Annual General Meeting may be challenged in court, following the provisions of the general procedural law, in the following situations:*

a) *When such decisions are contrary to the law or to the Community Statutes.*

b) *When they are seriously damaging to the interests of the community itself and benefit one or several owners.*

c) *When they cause serious harm to an owner who has no legal obligation to suffer this harm, or when the decisions have been made by abusing the law.*

*2. Owners who expressly registered a dissenting vote in the meeting, those who were absent for any reason, and those who were incorrectly deprived of their right to vote are legally entitled to impugn these decisions. To challenge a resolution of the Meeting, an owner must be current in his payment of debts owed to the Community or he must deposit the amount of the debt with the Court beforehand. This rule shall not apply when challenging a decision regarding the establishment or alteration of the participation shares referred to in Article 9.*

*3. The action lapses three months after the decision taken by the general meeting unless the decision is contrary to law or to the Community Statutes, in which case the period is one year. For those owners who were absent this period is counted from the date of notification of the decision according to the procedure set out in Article 9.*

*4. Impugning a decision of the general meeting does not suspend its being put into force unless the Court orders so, as a precautionary measure, at the petition of the plaintiff and having heard the community of owners.*

## WHAT IT MEANS

Article 18 means that even one owner can challenge a community decision in court, if it seriously harms the interests of one of the members, or if it seems to benefit a few people to the detriment of the community as a whole, or if it is contrary to law or the Statutes of the Community.

Dissenters, be warned that you must have your vote against the measure reflected in the official minutes book if you want to impugn the decision.

Absentees have three months in most cases, and they had better have their fees paid up.

## *ARTICLE 19.*

*1. Decisions of the general meeting shall be recorded in a book of minutes stamped and validated by the Property Registrar in the form set out by law.*

*2. The minutes of each meeting must express at least the following circumstances:*

*a) The date and place of the meeting*

*b) The name of the caller of the meeting, or the names of the owners who promoted it.*

*c) Whether it was ordinary or extraordinary and whether it was held on first or second call.*

*d) List of all those attending and their respective offices, as well as those owners represented by proxy, with the cuotas of each one.*

*e) The agenda for the meeting.*

*f) Decisions taken, showing, where it is relevant for the validity of the decision, the names of those owners who voted in favour and those who voted against them, as well as the participation shares they respectively represent.*

*3. The minutes book should close with the signatures of the president and the secretary at the end of the meeting or within ten days after. At the signing of the minutes book, the resolutions of the meeting shall be in force, unless the law disposes otherwise.*

*The minutes shall be sent to the absent owners, following the procedure set out in Article 9.*

*Errors or defects in the minutes are rectifiable, provided that the book unmistakeably indicates the date and place of the meeting, the owners in attendance, either present or represented by proxy, the decisions taken, with notation of the votes for and against, as well as the participation shares represented and that the book has been signed by the president and secretary. Said rectification should be made before the following general assembly, which must ratify the corrections.*

*4. The Secretary will keep the minutes books of the general meeting. He will likewise retain, during a period of five years, the convocations, communications, powers of attorney and other documents relating to the meetings.*

## WHAT IT MEANS

The official minutes book described here must be kept in Spanish because it is a legal document, registering the acts of the community. This *libro de actas* must be stamped by the Registrar of Property and its contents can be cited in court.

The book must record the names of the members and proxies present at the meeting; tell who presided; when and where the meeting was held; give the agenda for the meeting; mention the main points of view discussed in the debate; list the resolutions taken and record the voting results.

If any member or group wishes to contest a resolution of the community, either in person or by certified post, this also should be recorded.

This minutes book establishes the powers of the president and any other officer to act for the community, and justifies the actions by its recording of the community's votes.

The annual general meeting usually begins with the reading of the minutes of the previous meeting, which must be approved by the members. If any member has a protest against the book, it must be registered officially in the book itself. It sometimes happens that the official record does not agree with one persons version of what actually happened, so it is necessary to be attentive.

## *ARTICLE 20.*

*It is the function of the administrator:*

*a)   To ensure the proper management of the house, its installations and services and, to this effect, provide the owners with timely information and warnings.*

*b)   To prepare the budget of anticipated expenses sufficiently in advance and submit it to the general meeting, proposing the necessary measures to cover the expenses.*

*c)   To attend to the conservation and maintenance of the building, arranging for the ordinary repairs and taking urgent measures regarding extraordinary repairs, giving an immediate report to the general meeting or, as the case may be, to the property owners.*

*d)   To carry out resolutions taken regarding works and to make any payments and receive any monies as properly disposed.*

*e)   To act, when the case arises, as secretary of the general meeting and to keep custody, at the disposition of the owners, of the documentation of the community.*

*f)   Any other functions conferred by the general meeting.*

## WHAT IT MEANS

Contrary to popular belief, the administrator, when he is a paid professional, is not an elected officer of the community. He is contracted for his services, usually for one year, and the community may choose not to renew his contract at its termination, and to employ another paid professional administrator.

Of course, a community member, the president or another, may carry out the many duties of administrating the building.

Article 20 lists the functions of the administrator. He must run the building properly and keep the owners informed about it. If there is no treasurer, the administrator prepares the budget for the coming year, attends to repairs in the building, makes payments and receives money, acts as secretary and keeps the community records safe and at the disposition of the members, and any other functions voted to him by the community.

Because the administrator may be a volunteer member of the community, the law sets no requirement for carrying out this mission. The administrator needs no professional title or special qualifications. He does not have to be Spanish or even to speak Spanish.

Nevertheless, many of the paid professional administrators hold titles as lawyers, gestors or, best of all, as an *administrador de fincas*, a professional property management expert.

Most administrators try to give good service to the community, charge reasonable fees, and put up with many petty complaints from the members. But others are not so honest, and more than one community has had bad experiences with administrators who seem to feel that the community works for them, rather than the other way around.

Sometimes promoters, in order to maintain their influence in the community, even have the names of administrators written into the original community statutes when they register the building. They are counting on the fact that any change in the statutes requires a unanimous vote, which is very difficult to achieve, so the members could not put out the administrator. Their legal position here is quite shaky, though, as the law also says that the annual general meeting has the power to change the president and the administrator.

In any case, if the community feels that the administrator is not presenting proper accounts, or his fees are too high, or he has purchased supplies from his cousin when he could have got them more cheaply from another source, they can vote him out.

The administrator, whether professional or volunteer, can also be sued in court for damages caused by his misconduct or negligence in office.

## *ARTICLE 21.*

*1. The obligations referred to in paragraphs e) and f) of Article 9 must be fulfilled by the owner of the flat or premises in the time and form determined by the General Meeting. If not, the President or the Administrator, if so disposed by the General Meeting, can seek legal redress by the procedure established in this Article.*

*2. Use of this procedure will require the prior notification of the decision of the General Meeting approving the claim of the debt with the Community by the person acting as Secretary, with the endorsement of the President, providing that this decision has been notified to the owners affected in the form set out in Article 9.*

*3. Territorial jurisdiction shall correspond exclusively to the Court of the place where the property is located. Representation by a lawyer or procurator shall not be compulsory, subject to the dispositions of paragraph 10. of this Article.*

*4. Proceedings begin with a simple claim form, accompanied by the certification referred to in Number 2. of this Article. In case the previous owner of the property is liable jointly for the debt, without affecting his right to claim repayment from the present owner, action should be brought against him jointly with the present owner. In any case, the action must be brought against the registered owner.*

*5. Once the claim has been presented and accepted for procedure, the judge shall summon the defendant and order him to pay the plaintiff within 20 days and accredit this to the Court, or to appear before the court and present his allegations justifying that he does not owe, either in whole or in part, the amount claimed. The summons should be served at the domicile in Spain previously designated by the debtor, or in its absence, at the flat itself, with the admonition that, if he neither pays nor appears to declare his reasons for re-*

THE SPANISH PROPERTY GUIDE

*fusal to pay, the court will rule against him in the manner set out in the following Number.*

*6. If the defendant does not appear before the Court and does not oppose the claim, the Judge shall issue a writ of execution which shall proceed according to the provisions for court rulings, for the amount owed plus interest and foreseeable costs and for prior extrajudicial costs for the notifications of the debt if the services of a Notary were used.*

*The plaintiff in this procedure and the debtor acted against shall not be able to respectively claim the amount or seek the refund of monies paid out in a subsequent ordinary civil action.*

*From the time the writ is issued, the debt will draw interest at the legal interest rate plus two per cent.*

*7. If the debtor pays upon the demand for payment, as soon as he accredits this to the court, he will be given the document registering the debt and the case will be dropped.*

*Nevertheless, the legal costs cited in Number 10 of this Article and the expenses set out in the preceding Number will be for his account.*

*8. If the debtor opposes the claim, giving reasons for refusal to pay, in whole or in part, the Judge, after transmitting the opposition plea to the plaintiff, shall follow the procedure for oral hearings from the time of the summons. However, once opposition is declared, the plaintiff may seek a lien or attachment on assets of the debtor of sufficient value to cover the amount claimed, interest, and costs.*

*The Judge will dispose such lien in any case without the necessity of the creditor posting bond. The debtor can avoid the lien by presenting a bank guarantee for the amount set in the preventive lien.*

*9. If the debtor appears on time in court and opposes the payment only in part, alleging overcharging, his plea will be admitted only when he accredits having either paid or placed at the disposition of the plaintiff, before the claim was made, the amount he recognizes as his debt. If the opposition is based on overcharging, the lien can only be sought for the amount not paid by the debtor.*

240

*10. The court's ruling will have the force of "final judgment"*

*Costs will be charged to the party whose claim is totally rejected. If the claim is partially granted, each party will pay its own individual costs and half of the common costs. The order to pay costs will include legal fees to lawyer and procurator of the winning side, if they have used these professional services in their claim or opposition.*

*11. Community fees which fall due while the case is in process can be added to the amount without having to recommence the proceedings, considering them as common to the debt and affected by the procedural stages which went before. This faculty shall extend through the execution of the writ.*

*This addition during the process of community fees falling due after the presentation of the claim shall require prior accreditation by a new certification of the community decision approving the claim, issued according to the provisions of Number 2.*

*12, No appeal against the ruling will be admitted to court unless the defendant accredits having settled the debt or deposited the amount of the judgment with the court before he brings the appeal.*

*If the ruling orders the payment of certain sums for late payment or for unpaid fees due, the appeal will be annulled if the appellant ceases to pay or to deposit with the court on time the payments of the same class which continue to come due during the procedure.*

## WHAT IT MEANS

This article sets out the real changes in the new 1999 law. A law with some teeth in it.

The community can now certify the debt and go immediately into court for a lien against the debtor's property. If the debtor does not pay up, the court will order some of his assets seized to pay the debt. If the debtor chooses to fight the bill, he himself must put up either his assets or a bank guarantee for the amount. Formerly, the community was required to make a deposit with the court when they sought to collect the back fees. No longer.

Furthermore, any community debts that accumulate during the procedure are simply added into the original debt. No complications.

Furthermore, if the debtor fights to drag out the case, he will be liable for the community's legal costs if he loses.

This new tool for collecting Community debts has proven so effective that, in less than a year, more than 40 per cent of all outstanding Community fees in Spain have been collected, most of them simply on the threat of going to court.

## *ARTICLE 22*

*1. The Community of Property Owners will be liable with all its assets and credits for any debt to third parties. In addition, the creditor can act against each individual owner who took part in the process for his proportional share of the unpaid amount, after serving a demand for payment on such owners.*

*2. Any owner can oppose the claim by justifying that he is fully current in the payment of all debts due to the community at the time the demand referred to above was made.*

*If the debtor immediately pays the demand, he will be charged the proportional part of the costs involved.*

## WHAT IT MEANS

It happens with a certain frequency that Communities of Property Owners cannot pay their debts to suppliers or service providers simply because their members have not paid their annual Community fees.

This Article gives Community creditors a handle on direct action. They can proceed against the members themselves as individuals. Those members who are fully paid up, however, cannot be made to pay.

## ARTICLE 23

*The legal structure of horizontal property (condominium) is terminated:*

*1. By the destruction of the building, unless there is agreement to the contrary.*

*Such destruction shall be deemed to exist when the cost of rebuilding exceeds fifty per cent of the value of the property at the time the event occurs, unless the amount in excess of the aforesaid cost is covered by insurance.*

*2. By conversion into ordinary ownership or joint ownership.*

## WHAT IT MEANS

Clearly, the horizontal property scheme must be terminated when the building is destroyed. By fire, for example. The second paragraph refers to the sale of the building to one owner or several joint owners. Yes, the community can even vote — unanimously, of course — to sell itself and divide the cash among the owners.

---

### CHAPTER III

---

### Regarding Private Real Estate Complexes

*ARTICLE 24.*

*1. The special scheme of property ownership set out in Article 396 of the Civil Code shall be applicable to those private real estate complexes which meet the following requirements:*

*a) Being made up of two or more buildings or independent plots whose principal use is dwellings or commercial premises.*

*b) The owners of these buildings or properties or of the units into which they are divided horizontally, with an inherent nature for this right, participate in an indivisible co-ownership of other real estate elements, such as roads, installations or services.*

2. *Private real estate complexes referred to in the previous Number may:*

a) *Constitute themselves as one only Community of Owners by means of any of the procedures established in the second paragraph of Article 5. In this case they will be subject to the dispositions of this Law, which will be fully applied to them.*

b) *Constitute themselves as a grouping of Communities of Owners. To this effect, the Charter of Constitution of the new grouped Community must be granted by the only and single owner of the complex or by the Presidents of all the Communities to compose it, previously authorised by majority vote of their respective general meetings. The Charter of Constitution will contain the description of the real estate complex in its setting and descriptions of the elements, roads, installations and common services. Likewise, it will fix the participation shares (cuotas) of each of the component Communities, which will be jointly liable for the obligation to contribute to the general expenses of the group macro-community. This title of charter and the Statutes of the Community can be inscribed in the Property Registry.*

3. *The grouping of Communities referred to above shall, to all effects, enjoy the same legal situation as Communities of Owners and will be governed by the dispositions of this Law, with the following special provisions:*

a) *The general assembly of owners , unless otherwise agreed, will be composed of the Presidents of the communities forming the group, who will represent the individual owners of each Community .*

b) *The making of decisions for which the Law requires qualified majorities will require, in all cases, the prior vote of the majority required in each of the individual Communities that compose the grouping.*

c) *Except by agreement of the general meeting otherwise, the dispositions of Article 9 of this Law regarding the reserve fund shall not apply to the group community.*

*The jurisdiction of the governing organs of the group community cover only the real estate elements, roads, installations and common services. In no case shall their decisions prejudice the faculties corresponding to the governing bodies of the Communities of Owners which make up the grouping of Communities.*

*4. The dispositions of this Law, with the same special provisions, shall be applicable to those private real estate complexes which do not adopt any of the legal forms indicated in Number 2 as a complement to agreements made by the co-owners among themselves*

## WHAT IT MEANS

This is the big one. For the first time, the Horizontal Law takes account of urbanisations of detached houses, or groupings of townhouses, flats and detached villas.

The full protection of the new Horizontal Law is now available for these urbanisations, with very little effort on their part. They can vote for it, write themselves a set of Statutes, and go straight to the Property Registry.

Until now, urbanisations had to form themselves as Collaborating Urbanistic Entities, a complex process which often proved extremely expensive for the owners and involved long and tortuous negotiations with the Town Hall.

Sometimes the formation of an EUC will be the only possibility for an urbanisation, but many of them will now find their way smoothed to legality, and the capacity to enforce debt collection.

## ADDITIONAL DISPOSITION.

*1. Without prejudice to any dispositions which, using the powers conferred on them, the Regional Governments may make, the constitution of the reserve fund regulated in Article 9.1.f) shall comply with the following rules:*

*a) The fund must be created when the General Meeting approves the ordinary yearly budget, corresponding to the year immediately following the putting into effect of this Law.*

*New Communities shall create the fund when they approve their first ordinary budget.*

b) *When constituted, the fund shall be endowed with no less than 2.5 per cent of the ordinary budget of the Community. To this effect, the owners must make in advance the necessary contributions proportionally to their participation shares.*

c) *When the ordinary budget for the financial year following that in which the fund was established is passed, the amount of the reserve fund should reach the minimum quantity established in Article 9.*

*2. The amount of the reserve fund at no time during the budget period shall be less than the minimum legally established.*

*Amounts drawn from the reserve fund during the budget period in order to pay the expenses on maintenance and repairs of the property permitted by the present law shall be computed as an integral part of the fund for purposes of calculating its minimum amount.*

*At the beginning of the following financial year there shall be made the contributions necessary to cover the amounts drawn from the reserve fund in accordance with the terms of the preceding paragraph.*

# Communities of Detached Villas

THOSE WHO LIVE in urbanisations of detached villas have a more complicated set of problems than those living in flats. Before 1978 it was very difficult for them to form any sort of community with the legal power to enforce its statutes and compel payment of fees.

The inhabitants of these housing estates, or urbanisations, a rather new invention in Spain at that time, had to find ways of financing their roads, lighting, security, gardens, etc., as well as establishing the basic services of water, electric power and rubbish collection.

Even when they can now come under the protection of the Horizontal Law, they still have these basic problems not related to the pure legality of their existence.

In addition, the urbanisations often had complex relations with the Town Hall of their municipality. If the road passing through the estate continues on to other properties and is used by the general public, who pays for its maintenance?

Can the inhabitants cut this road and seal off the community, or are they obliged to permit the public to use it?

Will the Town Hall rubbish collectors enter the estate, or must all rubbish be placed at a central point for collection?

A thousand questions arise.

What is basically important for the formation of a community is Royal Decree 3288/1978 of August 25, which sets forth the regulations for urban administration based on the existing *Ley del Suelo*, the Land Law. Even the 1978 regulations are complex and confusing, but they can provide a framework for setting up an effective community.

These regulations establish the figure of the *Entidad Urbanistica Colaboradora de Gestión y Conservación,* the Collaborating Urbanistic Entity of Maintenance and Management. A real mouthful to describe the quasi-public functions of the urbanisation of detached villas. This is often shortened today to EUC.

In a perfect world, you would find that your dream villa was located on an urbanisation where all roads, lighting and services were carefully provided by a benevolent and foresighted municipal administration, just as they are in many countries. But you are more likely to encounter a situation where the developer is no longer maintaining the roads and services, where the Town Hall refuses to help because all the requirements in the original building permission were not fulfilled by the developers, and the owners are unable to establish an effective community.

You need to start with Article 25 of the 1978 regulations. If you are lucky, your situation will come under Section 3 of this law which provides for the forming of collaborating entities which group all owners in a certain zone, whether they want to join or not. Without the power to compel all owners to belong to the entity, it would be meaningless.

Then you can study Article 67, which provides that the Town Hall will take charge of maintaining and providing all normal services once these have been ceded to the Town Hall. That is, the association of owners or the developer will transfer the roads, sewage, lighting and perhaps some common green zone to the Town Hall.

The catch here is that the Town Hall may very well refuse to accept this transfer until the roads and other services have been put into good condition. Guess who must pay for this. Right. Either the developer, or the owners as a group. Some parts of the regulations can even oblige the urbanisation to pay all costs for establishing connections to the nearest town roads, sewers and lighting systems.

The great advantage of the collaborating entity is that the urbanisation then becomes a normal part of the municipality for the provision of basic services, and, if one of the members refuses to pay his share of community fees, the Town Hall itself may act against him with the threat to seize his property or bank account to satisfy the unpaid debt. This procedure is much more effective and rapid than going through the courts.

So you begin to see that the collaborating entity must work closely with the municipal authorities because the urbanisation is not separated from the rest of the world the way an apartment building is.

In fact, the authorization of the Town Hall is required for the formation of this entity.

All these negotiations between the owners and the municipal authorities will require the counsel and representation of a Spanish lawyer or property administrator who is knowledgeable in this area.

In one recent case on the Costa del Sol, the backers of a very large estate worked closely with the existing owners and the Town Hall.

First the existing owners voted unanimously to form an association. Then the developers, acting on the requirements of the Town Hall, put all the services in good order. Costs were shared by the owners and the developer.

Then the backers had to pay the Town Hall a fine of 20 million pesetas for not fulfilling all their original obligations. (The Town Hall first wanted 80 million pesetas, but were argued into the lower figure.)

Finally, the Town Hall accepted the transfer of the roads and other services, and authorized the formation of a collaborating urban entity. This was properly registered in the registry of such entities, which exists at the provincial urban office, giving it a legal personality.

Any new purchaser in this zone must now become a member of the entity by virtue of his purchase. This is clearly stated in each sales contract. Both the developer and the present owners have bound themselves to include such a clause in any sales deed. Even if they didn't, the legal personality of the entity requires it.

Now the members only have to squabble among themselves about how much to pay for the security patrol, whether they want an extra tennis court and how to act against the owner with the barking dogs. Of course they also have to fight with their new partners in the Town Hall about the size of their assessment for the sewage repairs, compared to the urbanisation just down the road. The problems will never end, but at least they have a clear and coherent system for dealing with them.

These particular members are now up in arms because they feel they are being charged twice for municipal services. That is because they pay their annual real estate taxes to the Town Hall, the IBI, just like other owners. But they also pay their annual fees to the EUC, which, they argue, covers basically the same services, so they are being forced to pay twice. The argument is still going on.

Things can be much worse in a situation where the owners cannot agree at the beginning and where the developer is not willing to help. But if the whole thing seems like too much trouble, remember that a well-run community can add millions of pesetas to your property's value and a poorly-maintained urbanisation can cut millions off your price.

The following section contains an English translation of Spanish regulations affecting the formation of conservation entities. It is not complete because many different bodies of law can come into play, but it gives a good idea of the legislation.

# LAW FOR DETACHED VILLAS, IN ENGLISH

Land Law Regulations
III
Regulations of Urban Administration

*TITLE I General Dispositions*

## CHAPTER 1. Subjects and Means of Administration
## SECTION 6.

### ARTICLE 24.

*1. Affected parties may participate in urban administration through the creation of Collaborating Urban Entities.*

*2. Collaborating Urban Entities are:*

*a) Compensation Boards.*

*b) Administrative Associations of owners in the co-operation system.*

*c) Entities of Conservation.*

*3. Collaborating Urban Entities will be governed by their Statutes and by the dispositions of this section, without prejudice to the application of the specific precepts contained in Chapters 11 and III of Title V of these Regulations for Compensation Boards and Administrative Associations of owners in the co-operation system, nor to the provisions established in Chapter 1-V of Title III for the conservation of the works of urbanisation.*

### WHAT IT MEANS

These regulations establish a legal basis for private citizens to participate in public administration. Keep in mind that streets, lighting, main drains, sewage systems and electric conduits passing through the land of the urbanisation to the next property will be of public nature. It is not like a building of flats, in which the services are simply connected and do not pass on to other properties.

This article of the regulations allows private persons to share administration of these services with the municipal authorities through the formation of one of three types of collaborating urban entities.

The first mentioned, the compensation board, is created when land is being re-zoned or subdivided and where several owners may be involved. The situation can get complicated. Imagine an area which includes a large working farm, a small factory with lots of land around it, nine or 10 homes built on large rural plots, and maybe a developer who has bought a big tract which he wants to urbanize. The nearby town is expanding and a new road is being put in. The entire zone will be declared building land.

The compensation board is the legal structure created for the purpose of sorting out all the problems that will arise and for seeing that each participant is fairly treated. The Town Hall is represented, too, as it will be expropriating land from some of the owners for the road and other services. The members of the board will squabble and negotiate until they agree on each party's share of the rights and obligations. This is one form of urban entity.

The compensation board operates principally as a forum to ensure the equitable distribution of problems and profits in such a re-zoning situation. But what happens after the subdivision is complete?

One scheme set up in law is the second structure mentioned in this article: the administrative association of owners in the co-operation system. Here the owners co-operate with each other and with the Town Hall to organize smooth functioning of the services in the area they share. This is much like the conservation entity, but its legal underpinnings are different, involving several different ownerships.

Both the compensation board and the administrative association are designed to serve in the early stages of a transformation in the ownership pattern of land. Either of them can be changed into a conservation entity, the legal framework for the ongoing maintenance of an established urbanisation.

## ARTICLE 25.

*1. The constitution of the Compensation Boards and of the Administrative Associations of owners in the co-operation system shall be adapted to the provisions of the regulations contained in the respective schemes of action.*

*2. Entities of conservation of the works of urbanisation may be constituted as a result of the transformation of some preexisting Entity of those set out in the previous number or, specifically for these purposes, without previously having constituted any Entity for the execution of the works of urbanisation.*

*3. The constitution of a conservation Entity will be obligatory whenever the duty of conservation of the works of urbanisation falls upon the owners included in a determined zone or unit of action by virtue of the dispositions of the town urban Plan or the bases of the urban action programme or if it results expressly from legal dispositions. In such cases membership in the conservation entity will be obligatory for all owners included in its territorial range.*

## WHAT IT MEANS

The big news comes here in the last sentence of paragraph 3, which provides that membership in the conservation entity shall be obligatory for all owners in the zone, and that the formation of the conservation entity shall be obligatory when provided by law, meaning that it may be set out in the town urban development plan, or in a Plan of Urbantistic Action, a development plan for a restricted area, or it may simply be a regulation passed by the Town Council. Any legal disposition will suffice.

In practice this means some urbanisations will find that the law requires them to form a conservation entity and that all must be members, and other urbanisations will find it is not legally necessary for them to do so.

## ARTICLE 26.

*1. Collaborating urbanistic Entities shall have an administrative character and shall be dependent in this order on the acting urbanistic Administration.*

*2. The legal personality of collaborating urbanistic Entities shall be understood as acquired from the moment of their inscription in the corresponding Registry.*

### WHAT IT MEANS

The first paragraph of this article grants to these entities powers to act legally, and notes that this power depends on the entity's relation to the public administration involved, which would usually be the municipality, though it could also be the province or a special authority ruling some particular piece of terrain.

The second paragraph reminds us that there exists a special Registry for these entities and they cannot act with legal force, to compel payment of debts, for example, until the entity is properly registered.

## ARTICLE 27.

*1. The constitution of collaborating urban entities, as well as their Statutes, must be approved by the acting urban Administration.*

*2. The document approving this constitution shall be entered in the Registry of Collaborating Urban Entities which is kept by the respective Provincial Urban Commissions, where likewise shall be kept an example of the statutes of the entity authorized by the competent official.*

*3. The appointments and dismissals of the persons charged with governing and administrating the entity shall also be inscribed in said Registry.*

*4. Modification of the statutes shall require the approval of the acting urban Administration. The respective resolutions, with the content of the modification, in such case, must be entered in the Registry.*

## WHAT IT MEANS

This article points up the importance of the cooperation required of the local Town Hall or other urban administration body which has competence over the zone. These official bodies must approve the formation of the entity and its statutes.

The names of its officers, and any changes in its rules, must be registered in the Registry. Any major changes of the statutes will require approval from the municipal authorities.

## *ARTICLE 28.*

*The transfer of title which determines membership in any of the types of collaborating urbanistic entities shall carry with it the termination of the rights and obligations of the transferring party and the acquirer shall be understood as incorporated into the Entity from the time of transfer.*

## WHAT IT MEANS

This of course applies only when the Entity is legally constituted and registered. If the owner's community is not an Entity, but only a civil association, then each new buyer's contract must contain a clause stating that he joins the community and agrees to abide by its statutes.

## *ARTICLE 29.*

*Resolutions of collaborating urbanistic Entities shall be adopted by simple majority of participation shares, unless a special quorum is established in the Statutes or other regulations for certain cases. Such resolutions can be impugned in appeal to the acting urbanistic Administration.*

## WHAT IT MEANS

Each urban entity can make its own statutes with provisions on where unanimous vote may be required. If they do not, this article of the regulations will apply and a simple majority decision will be sufficient to take action. Any owner who feels his interests have been prejudiced can appeal the vote to the Town Hall or other official administration acting in the case.

## ARTICLES 30 THROUGH 57

Are of a highly technical nature and do not bear directly on the formation of communities.

## *ARTICLE 58.*

*The owners of properties affected by an urbanistic action programme shall be obliged to pay the costs of urbanisation specified in the following articles in proportion to the area of their respective properties, or, as the case may be, to the area figuring in the documents referred to in Article 53 of these regulations.*

## WHAT IT MEANS

This means that owners shall be assessed payment participation shares according to the size of their properties. Big properties pay more, small properties pay less. The Article 53 referred to relates to various forms of documenting property ownership, such as the *Registro de la Propiedad*, and others.

## *ARTICLE 59.*

*1. The cost of works of urbanisation which are charged to the account of the owners of a determined zone or unit of action shall include the following:*

a) *Street works, including works of levelling, compacting and paving of roadways, construction and kerbing of pavements and channelling which must be constructed in the subsurface of the public way for services.*

b) *Sanitation works, which include general and partial collectors, connections, sewers and culverts for rain-waters and purification installations, in the proportion that they affect the action unit or zone.*

c) *Water supply, in which is included works of obtaining the water, when such are necessary, the distribution to homes of potable water, of irrigation water and of fluid for fire-fighting.*

d) *Supply of electrical current, including its conduction and distribution and public lighting.*

*e) Gardening and tree-planting in parks, gardens and public ways.*

*2. Private parties involved in works of urbanisation in a zone or urban action unit may be reimbursed for the expenses of installation of the networks of supply of water and electricity, charged to the concession-holding companies, to the extent that, according to the regulation of such services, these expenses must not be charged to the users. The costs of installation shall be accredited by certification issued by the acting administration.*

## WHAT IT MEANS

Have they left anything out? The owners on an urbanisation can find themselves liable for any of the expenses mentioned here. If the developer has failed to carry out all requirements set by the Town Hall, either in the urban plan itself or other subsidiary legislation, the owners can be stuck for it in most cases. It pays to check up first.

## *ARTICLE 60.*

*Any indemnities owed to the owners and renters of buildings or constructions of any sort which must be knocked down for the correct execution of the plan, as well as indemnity payments arising from the destruction of plantings, works or installations incompatible with the plan being carried out shall likewise be charged to the account of the property owners in the proportions set out in Article 58.*

## WHAT IT MEANS

Yes, they left something out. Owners are also liable for any payments made to persons suffering loss from the execution of the urbanisation plan.

## *ARTICLE 61.*

*Also for the account of the owners of land included in the zone or relevant action unit shall be the cost of preparing and processing the Plan of plots and the projects of urbanisation and the total cost of expenses of subdivision or compensation.*

## WHAT IT MEANS

This expense would fall on the owners of land which is in the process of being subdivided, and will produce profits for them when they sell. It is not likely to affect purchasers on an already-established urbanisation; but be alert because legal expenses can also be charged to the owners.

## ARTICLE 62.

*If agreement exists between the Administration and the affected owners, the payment of all or part of the expenses noted in the three previous articles can be made by the owners ceding to the Administration, for no consideration and free of all charges, buildable land in the amount deemed sufficient for the compensation of such expenses, whose value shall be determined in the agreement itself.*

## WHAT IT MEANS

That's good of the administration. If you can't pay, they will accept your valuable land instead. In fact, this situation normally arises when the town itself is re-zoning land. The new building permissions mean large profits for the existing owners so it is expected they pay for it, either in cash or by the transfer of part of the land to the Town Hall.

## ARTICLE 63.

*Owners of non-programmed developable land which is the object of a Programme of urbanistic action, besides paying the costs of urbanisation set out in the previous articles and satisfying any supplementary charges which the programme may impose on them, must pay for the complete execution or the supplement necessary for the exterior works of infrastructure on which the urbanistic action is based, such as road networks connecting with population centres, installation or amplification of the channels of services of water supply, drains and sewage, purification stations, supply of electricity and any other services necessary for the land subject to the urbanistic action programme to be duly connected through these general systems with the structure of the Municipality in which the programme is carried out.*

## WHAT IT MEANS

Owners of land which is improved or made more valuable by any action of the Town Hall can find themselves liable even for these expenses.

## ARTICLE 64

Has been left out, as it does not bear directly on communities.

## *ARTICLE 65.*

*Incompliance by the owners of the land with the obligations and charges established in these Regulations will give rise to:*

a) *The collection of the urbanisation costs by executive order under threat of embargo and legal seizure of the property.*

b) *Expropriation by the Administration of the lands affected by compliance with the charges, the Administration itself, or the Compensation Board, as the case may be, being beneficiaries of the expropriation.*

## WHAT IT MEANS

This article is what makes the conservation entity such an effective form for communities of owners of detached villas in an urbanisation. The executive order to seize property of nonpayers is a far easier and swifter process than going to court against them, which can take many months, and even years.

## ARTICLE 66

Has been left out, as it does not bear directly on communities.

CHAPTER IV

# Maintenance of the Urbanisation

## ARTICLE 67.

*The conservation of the works of urbanisation and the maintenance of the equipment and installations of the public services will be the charge of the acting administration, once the transfer of these services has been made.*

## WHAT IT MEANS

Yes, this is the dream paradise in which the Town Hall provides and maintains all the basic services of the urbanisation. This article obliges them to do so. The catch is that they have to accept the transfer of these services from the private developer or urbanisation first. And they will not accept - and have not done so in many cases - these services until everything is properly installed and functioning. Sometimes this works quite well and the community, the services and the Town Hall co-operate in harmony happily ever after, with the occasional non-payer of fees being forced to produce the money by the threat of executive order. Far more often, the Town Hall finds many deficiencies in the installations and services and will not take over their administration and maintenance until the owners' community has put them right, at great expense. Be warned.

## ARTICLE 68.

*1. Regardless of the dispositions of the preceding article, the owners of the land included in the zone or action unit will be subject to the aforesaid obligation when it is imposed on them by the Urban Zoning Plan, or by the bases of a programme of urban action or results expressly from legal dispositions.*

*2. In the case of the preceding number, the owners must form themselves into an Entity of Conservation.*

## WHAT IT MEANS

Even though it is clear from both principle and law that the owners will be obliged to maintain the installations, this article exists to remind us of that fact. Even when no specific provision is made for this, that last phrase of Article 68 paragraph 1 - *"results expressly from legal dispositions"* - gives the Town Hall the power to pass a resolution requiring the owners to maintain their roads in good repair, and the community will be bound by law.

## ARTICLE 69.

*1. The participation of the owners in the obligation of conservation and maintenance of the works of urbanisation, equipment and installations of the public services, when this is not the charge of the acting administration, shall be determined as a function of the participation share set for them by the Compensation Board, in the subdivision plan, or, as the case may be, in the share specified in the Entity of Conservation.*

*2. If systems of horizontal property have been constituted over the properties, the contribution of the owners to said obligation of conservation and maintenance shall be determined by the participation share [cuotal with relation to the total value of the property which is assigned in each community.*

## WHAT IT MEANS

This article determines the way in which each owner's share of the payment is calculated, and provides also for calculating the shares of apartment dwellers who already have horizontal property systems operating in their buildings located on the parent urbanisation.

## ARTICLE 70.

*1. Whosoever shall be the subject to whom corresponds the obligation of maintenance referred to in the preceding articles, the Town Hall or the acting administration, in its condition as owner of the lands of public domain, works, equipment and installations of obligatory cession, may require by executive order under threat of embargo the payment of the*

*shares owed, whether acting on its own initiative or at the*
*instance of the collaborating urbanistic Entity.*

*2. The amount of the payment share will be delivered by*
*the Town Hall or acting administration to the Entity charged*
*with the conservation, when this obligation does not pertain*
*to the Administration.*

## WHAT IT MEANS

Paragraph 1 here repeats the power of the Town Hall to
carry out an executive order of garnishment or embargo in
order to compel payment of participation share fees. It notes
that the Town Hall may do this either on its own initiative
or when requested by the conservation entity.

Paragraph 2 makes it clear that the Town Hall is to
deliver this money to the conservation entity, unless the
Town Hall itself is charged with the maintenance of the services. This means the Town Hall can collect the money and
provide the services, or collect part of the money and provide part of the services.

Because the Town Hall itself is often a member of the entity, because of its own installations on the 10 per cent of
the land which the promoter must transfer to the Town,
this gives rise to a situation where the Town Hall may have
to collect debts from itself.

## "LEGALITY" OF COMMUNITIES

A final note here on the "legality" of communities. Through-
out this text we refer to the inscription of the community in
the Property Registry or Registry of Conservation Entities.
We point out that the Statutes must be registered in order
to be fully legal, and we insist on every point of the law
being observed.

This is all well and good. In the real world, however, we
find groups of houses built in the property boom that do not
really make up an urbanisation, where the owners have
simply agreed to organize and pay for some basic services
among themselves. We find urbanisations that were never
registered as such, where no community Statutes exist, but

the owners hold annual meetings and pay dues. We find other urbanisations, where the Community has formal Statutes and regulations, but these are not registered.

Are all these other forms of communities "legal"?

Well, in one sense they are not legal because they are not registered. But if you, as an owner in one of these situations, think you can get away with not paying your fees, perhaps you should think again.

Spanish courts have ruled on a number of occasions that these communities, although not registered, have acquired a legal personality simply by existing through the years, that they function for the benefit of the owners and society in general, and so they can in fact compel the payment of fees and bring a case against a non-payer, even seizing his property and having it sold at auction.

# Index

# D

# E

# F

# G

# H

# J

# L

# M

# N

# O

---

# P

---

---

# Q

---

---

# R

---

---

# S

---

SPECIAL TAX ON OFFSHORE COMPANIES 149
STATUTE OF LIMITATIONS 182
SUBASTA/SUBASTAS/SUBASTEROS 33, 50

## T

TASACIÓN 177
TAX HAVENS 47, 149
TEMPORADA CONTRACT 109
TESTAMENTO ABIERTO 172
TESTAMENTO CERRADO 173
THE LAW REGULATING THE RIGHTS OF ROTATIONAL ENJOYMENT 60
TIMESHARE 59
TODOS LOS GASTOS 29
TOPOGRAFO 93
TRANSFER TAX 80
TRASPASO 117
TREASURER 224

## U

UNANIMITY 231
URBANISMO 25
USUFRUC/USUFRUCTO 141, 167, 183, 228

## V

VALOR CATASTRAL 21, 22, 83, 124
VICE-PRESIDENT 224
VIVIENDA CONTRACT 109
VIVIENDA DE PROTECCIÓN OFICIAL 65
VOTE 231, 232, 233

## W

WEALTH TAX 84, 125, 126
WILL 165

# MORE BOOKS FROM SANTANA

*You and the Law in Spain* Thousands of readers have relied on this best selling book to guide them through the Spanish legal jungle. Now, there is a new, completely revised edition with even more information on taxes, work permits, cars, banking, proper ty and lots more. It's a book no foreigner in Spain can afford to be without. *By David Searl. 224 pages.*

*Cooking in Spain* The definitive guide to cooking in Spain, with more than 400 great recipes. Complete information on regional specialities and culinary history, how to buy the best at the market, English-Spanish glossary and handy conversion guide. *By Janet Mendel. 376 Pages. Illustrated.*

*The Best of Spanish Cooking* The top food writer in Spain today invites you to a memorable feast featuring her all-time favourite Spanish recipes. More than 170 tantalizing dishes are presented, allowing you to recreate the flavour of Spain in your own home. *By Janet Mendel. 172 pages.*

*Tapas and More Great Dishes from Spain* This striking cookbook is a celebration of the sunny flavours of Spain - olive oil, garlic, fresh fruits and vegetables, meat and seafood -in an attractive presentation of 70 classic recipes and stunning colour photographs. *By Janet Mendel, Photographs by John James Wood. 88 pages*

*Expand Your Spanish* Tackle the dreaded Spanish subjunctive and chuckle at the same time? You can with this book. The author keeps you smiling as she leads you through the minefield of Spanish grammar. Not a language book in the conventional sense, but it will help you over the obstacles that put many people off learning the language. *By Linda Hall de Gonzalez. 240 pages. Illustrated.*

*Inside Andalusia* Author David Baird invites you to explore an Andalusia you never dreamt of, to meet its people, to discover dramatic scenery and fascinating fiestas. Illustrated with brilliant colour photographs. Winner of the National Award for Travel Writing. *By David Baird. 224 pages. Illustrated.*

***The Story of Spain*** The bold and dramatic history of Spain from the caves of Altamira to our present day. A story of kings and poets, saints and conquistadores, emperors and revolutionaries. The author has drawn on years of rigorous research to recreate the drama, excitement and pathos of crucial events in the history of the western world. *By Mark Williams. 272 pages. Illustrated.*

***Andalusian Landscapes*** This outstanding book of colour pho tographs is a celebration of the astonishing collage of colours and textures in the Andalusian landscape. It captures the charm of remote villages and lonely farmhouses, fields ablaze with sun flowers and meadows full of poppies, the play of light on olive groves and the sun on the high sierras. *By Tim Gartside. 78 pages.*

***Birds of Iberia*** Detailed descriptions of more than 150 bird species and the main habitats, migration patterns and ornithological sites. Lavishly illustrated with fine line drawings and full-colour photographs. *By Clive Finlayson and David Tomlinson. 224 pages. Large format hardback. Illustrated.*

***Gardening in Spain*** Your most valuable tool for successful gardening in Spain. How to plan your garden, what to plant, when and how plant it, how to make the most of flowers, trees, shrubs, herbs. *By Marcelle Pitt. 216 pages. Illustrated.*

***A Selection of Wildflowers of Southern Spain*** Southern Spain is host to a rich variety of wildflowers in widely diverse habitats, some species growing nowhere else. This book describes more than 200 common plants of the region, each illustrated in full colour with simple text for easy identification and enjoyment. *By Betty Molesworth Allen. 260 pages. Illustrated*

***Shopping for Food and Wine in Spain*** Spain, though now an integral part of the European market, is still, happily, a little exotic. The foods and wines you find in Spanish markets are not always what you see back home. This complete guide tells you how to shop in Spain with confidence - saving you money, time and frustration. 176 pages.

***Caring for Your Pet in Spain*** A practical guide written hy experts that tells foreign residents how to protect their dogs and cats and other pets from unfamiliar diseases and create an environment in which their pets can live happy and healthy lives in Spain. *By Erny and Peter Harrison. 144 pages.*

**David the Dogman's A-Z Guide to DOGS**   More than 300 entries on everything you ever wanted to know about Man's best friend. Articles by world experts. Plus a full listing Internet Guide to over 250 top canine web sites. *By David Klein, 335 pages*.

**Ventas**   This unique guide reviews 55 great places where you can eat good hearty food in a country setting at half the price you would pay in a conventional restaurant - and all within a short drive of the Costa del Sol. *By Bob Carrick. 144 pages*.